GW00643553

CRICKET CONTEST
1979-80

CRICKET CONTEST

1979-80

The Post-Packer Tests

CHRISTOPHER MARTIN-JENKINS

Queen Anne Press
Macdonald Futura Publishers
London

First published in 1980 in Great Britain by
Queen Anne Press · London and Sydney

Macdonald Futura Publishers
Paulton House
8 Shepherdess Walk
London N1 7LW

ISBN 0 354 04507 5

Printed and bound in Great Britain by
Purnell and Sons Limited
Paulton (Bristol) and London

To Graham, Shelagh, Andrew and Peter

CONTENTS

ACKNOWLEDGEMENTS

I owe grateful thanks to the BBC for allowing me to write about, as well as to speak about, a season in Australia which was exhausting but never dull; and I again want to thank Patrick Allen for compiling the copious statistical section, and Patrick Eagar and Ron McKenzie of the *Mirror/Australian/Telegraph* publications group for supplying the excellent photographs. Ron McKenzie took all the photographs up to and including the Lillee sequence, with the exception of those of Croft and Kallicharran; Patrick Eagar was responsible for these two and all the remaining photographs in the book.

Chapter One
BIRTH OF THE NEW ORDER

To say that the 1979-80 cricket season in Australia was unique is not quite true. The programme of international limited-over games and Test matches was certainly unlike anything previously organised by the Australian Cricket Board, but it bore a strong resemblance to the matches arranged in opposition to the Board in the previous two years by the Kerry Packer organisation, World Series Cricket. The prolonged and bitter rivalry between the Board and WSC had ended officially on 30 May 1979 when the ACB chairman Bob Parish and the managing director of WSC Lynton Taylor made a joint declaration of their intention to work together in future.

It is pointless now to speculate on what might have happened had the Australian Board 'sweated it out' for one more season. World Series Cricket had initially been envisaged as a three-year experiment, and most of the players were contracted for one more year when the peace treaty with the Board was made. The Board had bitterly opposed WSC from the outset: most of the best Australian players had been whisked off by offers of relatively huge salaries, and many spectators were wooed away from the Board matches by the attractively packaged rival product. This seriously affected the Board's financial well-being. Not only was it forced to pay the unestablished cricketers now representing Australia much more than it had previously paid the 'defectors', but because those players were less famous and because they were so soundly beaten (5-1) by England in the Ashes series of 1978-79 the gates for traditional matches were relatively poor and money was lost. In the two years of WSC the Board lost $810,000 (some £400,000) and WSC's losses were also substantial. Neither side was gaining anything from the war: the WSC players were a good deal more satisfied by their pay packets than they were by the artificial and glossily dressed cricket they were playing, and from Mr Packer's personal point of view the object he had always had in mind when setting up his rival promotion – the contract to televise Test matches – had still not been obtained. There was therefore a strong incentive on both sides to compromise. But what probably finally decided the senior officials of the Australian Board to swallow their pride and invite negotiations was the fact that they had very little with which to counteract the proposed third season of WSC. Their plans for 1979-80 were for India and England, who had both toured Australia in the last two years, to return for a triangular tournament of limited-over matches. They had little chance of selling such a programme to an Australian public which was already heartily sick of the civil war, and they knew it. Accordingly, during the first Test against Pakistan at Melbourne in February 1979, whilst the young Australian team was slipping towards another defeat before a miserable crowd lost in the vast concrete spaces of the Melbourne Cricket Ground, three Victorians with a firm control of the politics of the Board, Bob Parish, Ray Steele and Len Maddocks, entertained Kerry Packer himself to lunch in the plush basement dining-room of the Victoria Cricket Association. As the wine flowed – although the teetotal Mr Packer stuck to water – the first sweet words of compromise were spoken. When the rival generals emerged from the bowels of the MCG into daylight several hours later, red-faced and smiling, it was clear to everyone that an agreement was on the way. Sir Donald Bradman and the New South Welshman Tim Caldwell were later brought into the discussions, and the International Cricket Conference gave the ACB officials permission to work by themselves for a treaty which, of course, would have worldwide ramifications.

The agreement finally announced at the end of May marked the cessation of WSC matches and the 'paying-off' of the 68 players from Australia, West Indies, England and Pakistan under contract to them. WSC would continue as a marketing agent for its 'players, and its emblem would continue to be worn by Australian teams in limited-over internationals. But the major clause in the treaty was a ten-year agreement by the Board to grant Mr Packer's company, PBL Sports Ltd., (known hereafter as PBL), exclusive promotion rights to all matches arranged by the Board. This was widely believed to be worth £9 million ($1.7 million a year) to the Board, although the financial details of the treaty have remained strictly confidential. It surprised no one that Mr Packer's commercial television company Channel Nine had been granted sole television rights for three years, ahead of the Australian Broadcasting Commission, in whose defence the Board had originally defied Packer when first he had offered much more money for the television rights than the Government-financed ABC could afford. Two of the reasons originally given by the Board for sticking by the ABC and thus stinging Packer into his bitter, drastic and far-reaching action, were, first, that a commercial company could not bring cricket into the homes of all country areas as the ABC was able to do, and, second, that the latter had always stuck by cricket in good times and bad, televising the Sheffield Shield matches despite the fact that they lacked the glamour of Test matches. Ironically, not long after Channel Nine had finally got its contract it announced the amazing decision *not* to televise the early Sheffield Shield matches, despite the fact that, with 'established' players once again facing rivalry from the returning heroes from WSC, the start of the competition had a fascinating extra element.

The Board was at pains to announce in its statement that it had sole control over the selection of players for Tests and internationals and over the conduct of the game in Australia, not least the playing conditions. If this were wholly true, hitherto conservative officials might have been expected to reject most of the novelties which had been tried in the two years of WSC matches. On the contrary they were obliged by the terms of their agreement with PBL to become enthusiastic supporters of almost all of them, a fact which led to a less bitter but nevertheless serious argument between themselves and England's Test and County Cricket Board, who were fully supported by the England players.

Amongst the new ideas pushed by the Board at the behest of its new commercial 'allies' was the principle of having two touring sides to Australia each season instead of one, plus the staging of a World Cup *Test* series every four years in Australia. For the purposes of Channel Nine there was to be cricket at night as often as possible with the consequent use of white balls, black sightscreens and coloured clothing; and, much less understandably, it was proposed to make alterations to established playing customs which had stood the test of time. The agreement committed the ACB to using 'their best endeavours' to sell these ideas to other countries. England and the West Indies were asked, for example, to play Test matches without a rest day and limited-over matches *during daylight* with a white ball and black sightscreens. English officials were offended that limited-over cricket, which they had introduced with such success in county cricket as long ago as 1963, should suddenly be so glorified by an Australian Board which had hitherto accepted the attractions of this form of the game with very little enthusiasm. They were annoyed when the ACB tried to force upon them new rules used in WSC matches. These included circles drawn around the pitch outside which only a certain number of fielders were allowed to stand in the early stages of a match. The TCCB took the view that it had run with great success not only its own domestic limited-over competitions but also two Prudential World Cups. It rightly believed that it had learned from experience the good and bad lessons of this sort of cricket; the fewer the artificialities imposed on the game, it had found, the better.

There were other reasons for the sudden coolness in relations between the two Boards. The TCCB had stood by the ACB in its difficulties with Packer, had indeed footed most of the bill when the latter had successfully routed official attempts to ban his players by taking the matter to the High Court, and it felt that it therefore had a right to dictate some, at least, of the terms under which international cricket between the two countries should be played in future. The TCCB's strong preference was for a return to the old system of sending an England team to Australia every four years to play for the Ashes in a rubber of five or six Test matches, with several games before and during the series against State opposition. But English officials were keen to help to heal the wounds in Australian cricket and they had already agreed to send a team to Australia again in 1979-80. They therefore agreed to the PBL/ACB proposals that England should play three Tests against Australia, who would also play three against West Indies, with the three countries engaging in a triangular tournament of limited-over internationals. England successfully negotiated to reduce the number of the latter matches to eight played by each country with two teams emerging to play in a 'Grand Final' of three more matches – instead of five, as Australia had proposed originally.

The TCCB initially objected to a number of the. other Australian proposals. It was against the use of coloured clothing, pads and gloves for night cricket. These had originally been envisaged by the marketing men of WSC as a means of making the night game brighter for spectators and especially for television viewers. In fact, after initial hesitation, especially from the West Indians who had looked as though they were playing in pink pyjamas, the WSC players accepted the coloured clothes readily because they found that the white ball was easier to sight than it was against conventional whites. The TCCB agreed to experiment with coloured gear and the England players quickly decided, when they first practised under lights in Sydney during the opening week of their tour in early November, that they would be putting their opponents at a disadvantage if they wore white whilst the other teams had coloured gear. England drew the line, however, at the combination of white clothes with coloured stripes along the shoulders and thighs (like track-suits), which they rightly claimed was dressing up for the sake of it without in any way aiding the players. The West Indians had been reluctant to get into 'pyjamas' again, so the compromise reached meant that everyone would play in coloured pads and gloves – West Indies in maroon, Australia in yellow, England in blue – and whilst the other two teams wore striped shirts and trousers, England stayed in traditional white.

The promoters were in favour of these fancy clothes for largely non-cricketing reasons. They believed that the game was made more colourful for spectators both at the grounds and on television and they also had a strong interest in promoting new gear for their own commercial purposes. At the time of their agreement with the Board, WSC expected that some twenty firms would be involved in producing eighty or more different products such as sunhats, T-shirts, cricket bats and balls, cricket clothes, and scorebooks, which they expected would net more than £1 million in sales. Most items bore the WSC logo or a cuddly smurf-like figure called 'Stumpy', introduced to capture the very young in the cricket market. Children could have not only a teddy-bear substitute in Stumpy himself but ·also Stumpy jelly-babies and Stumpy ice-creams. 'The blossoming female interest in cricket,' as one of PBL's marketing men expressed it, would be catered for by sales of 'boob-tubes, sloppy Joes, fashion tops, tank tops, briefs, and towels': wouldn't *you* like to rub yourself down with a Rod Marsh towel? (Marsh seemed to be one of the most popular product endorsers: one T-shirt had a large pair of wicket-keeping gloves grasping the area of the bosom and was printed with the words 'Ooh Rodney!') Ladies (and men) could also buy gold or silver cricket bats and balls on a gold or silver chain – as worn by Dennis Lillee when he bowls. There was even a range of dog-coats 'for use when the time comes to take poodle for a wander'.

Returning to matters more strictly cricketing, an attempt was also made to introduce the white ball in daylight matches. Again it was argued that spectators, even in daylight, could see a white ball bowled by a fast bowler more clearly than a red one, whether they were watching on television or in the flesh. I think this is true but the players found that they had some difficulty in picking up the white ball at low level against the background of the white picket fences which mark Australian boundaries. The white ball meant also a black sightscreen, and there is a certain aesthetic pleasure in seeing white-clad figures, white sightscreens and white pickets against the greensward on a sunny day. Strictly from the players' point of view a red leather ball had served well enough for 200 years or so and there seemed little point in changing to suit the whims of television producers. In any case, red and green are at opposite ends of the colour spectrum. The England players practised with the white ball in their two limited-over games against Northern New South Wales in Newcastle (both of which they won) and found that the need to replace the ball after 25 overs when the new one became dirty was unsatisfactory because the replacement ball tended to be shinier and harder, thus making it difficult for spinners to grip at just the time they were likely to be introduced into the attack. England eventually – and after prolonged speculation – refused to use the white ball except in the day/night matches and also rejected an original Australian idea to have *two* new white balls, one at each end, so that the shine departed less quickly. The very fact that this should have been considered seriously underlines the inadequacy of the white ball. If the problem was that it became dirty so quickly, surely the better sighting qualities it possessed for a few overs were quickly invalidated?

The England team also successfully opposed attempts to impose sessions of more than three hours without intervals in day/night matches, and the hours of play for these games were settled, only four days before the first match, to begin at ten past two in the afternoon and finish before half-past ten at night, when Sydney's omnipotent lights had to be extinguished by law. To ensure that 50 overs a side were completed in this time, with an interval or dinner-break between innings and a 'flexible 20-minute interval' during each innings, the organisers suggested that there should be fines for slow over-rates, but this time it was the West Indians who refused to comply.

The West Indies team, however, with only five of their sixteen players unaccustomed to WSC cricket, were prepared to play their limited-over matches with the circle painted around the pitch behind which only two men were permitted to field in the first fifteen overs. It was clear to me that most of the ex-WSC players genuinely believed this to be an improvement on normal one-day rules because it forced captains to have an attacking field in the early part of the innings and prevented the side batting first from putting the fielders in defensive positions from the start if a big enough total had been achieved. But Mike Brearley, whose opinions in these matters generally carried more weight than anyone else's (and often more profound thought too), refused to put his side at a disadvantage by playing under rules to which it was unaccustomed. Prestige and a lot of money were at stake. These were not the matches in which to carry out experiments. Besides, said Brearley, the circles should instead be ovals, to follow the contours of the boundaries and allow mid-off and mid-on to stand in normal one-saving positions rather than in line with the stumps as they would playing for 'Ilford Catholic Club Third XI'. Brearley added, with a venom suggesting he had heard enough about white balls and circles: 'Australia and West Indies can play with green balls and hockey sticks if they like . . . our agreement was to play under existing laws if there was any disagreement.'

Professional cricketers are generally a conservative group of people. As for the Australian Board, it had for years been accused of burying its collective head in the sand. There was considerable irony, therefore, in its conversion, as swift as St Paul's on the road to Damascus, to the various experiments which it was now fervently pressing on behalf of its new commercial allies. I felt some sympathy for the Board officials, largely voluntary workers after all, who were first pushed by their declining finances into the arms of Packer's marketing men and who were now assailed on all sides: by the players for more money and more say in their own affairs; by the marketing experts for more changes and innovations; by the TCCB for a return to the satisfactory programme of cricket which had existed before the Revolution; and by the press for the disorganised start to the 1979-80 season which had begun with the rules for more than one competition unsettled, a collection of poorly attended warm-up matches for the visiting international teams, and a domestic limited-over competition – the McDonald's Cup – which, at least until the final at Melbourne, failed to arouse any special interest. In one match, for example, rain made a nonsense of the inflexible circles rule because Tasmania, batting second, were able to indulge in a chase for runs in a reduced number of overs with most of the fielders close to the wicket. Another game, the play-off for third place between Tasmania and Western Australia, was played at the Sydney Cricket Ground for the benefit of commercial television and since there was no local interest the echo of bat on ball from the empty stands aroused memories of the sparsely attended early matches in the first year of World Series Cricket. Perhaps, though, these were teething troubles, and mistakes were to be expected.

The ACB's semi-subservience to PBL was understandable if not entirely forgivable. He who pays the piper inevitably calls the tune; the Australian players had in the previous two years become used to doing and going whatever and wherever they were told provided the big pay-cheques kept arriving at the bank. Thus they accepted circles, striped clothes and the need to sell themselves in commercials because they believed that their new wealth depended on these things. Although they had formed a new Australian Cricketers' Association and talked much about player-power they had probably failed to realise the true *extent* of their power: Packer could not have achieved his coup without them.

If PBL were not exactly running Australian cricket they were effectively dictating policy, both to the players for whom they acted as agents and to the Board whose financial well-being now rested entirely on their historic contract with PBL. This was all in sharp contrast to the policy of cricket administrators in England towards the various sponsoring companies who were just as vital to the viability of first-class cricket there. Neither sponsors nor television companies in England have ever dictated the terms of any cricket competition. There is a school which maintains that cricket *must* in future be run by businessmen, not cricketers, if the game is to survive. But, in this case, who is to draw the line when they wish to change the game which has survived so long by itself? Are not businessmen in the game for their own good, rather than for that of cricketers?

Money was also at the root of the dispute which developed during a tough but courteous exchange of messages between Sydney and London in the weeks leading up to the tour. The problem with inviting two countries to tour was that both had to be guaranteed a profit. This put the Australian Board in difficulties from the start and they took a long time to satisfy their counterparts in England and the West Indies. In the end England settled for a very small profit of about £30,000, which, split between seventeen counties, made very little difference to the finances of the first-class clubs who were almost all reporting a bad year after a wet English summer during which most had been obliged to pay their players a minimum wage for the first time.

The TCCB felt strongly that, in view of its large income from PBL, the Australian Board might have been more generous. On the other hand, the more England asked to be paid for their tour, the more Australia would be likely to ask for the next tour of England. There was no point in being too greedy, though the TCCB was itself under pressure from two angles. The Test players made an attempt late in the 1979 season to increase their individual fees for the tour from the proposed sum of £6,500 basic, plus a further £200 for every past tour. In addition to this, most of the players who eventually made the trip had already received £2,500 from an 'option contract' which they had signed earlier in the year to keep themselves available for the winter tour. Thus, with abundant prize-money to play for as well, several members of the England team could expect to make in excess of £10,000 for their four months' work. This, however, many of the players felt to be inadequate, not by comparison with previous tours – because no English team had ever been paid so much before – but compared instead to the amounts likely to be made by their West Indian and Australian opponents, most of whom had been involved in World Series Cricket and thus had an additional year of their WSC salary to come, plus whatever extra their official governing bodies chose to give them. The situation was further complicated by the fact that three of the England players who were in the running for the tour, Derek Underwood, Bob Woolmer and Dennis Amiss, stood to earn a double payment – one from the TCCB and one from WSC – if they were picked. In the event only Underwood forced his way back into the side. Ironically, because of the ACB/PBL agreement, the Australian players – according to Lynton Taylor – did not get this 'double payment'; the money from the third year of their WSC contracts was paid instead by the ACB, who effectively 'leased' the WSC players. A similar arrangement was negotiated with the West Indians.

The pressure from the élite group of high-earning Test players on the TCCB was equalled by a strong pressure group at the bottom: the Cricketers' Association representing, in effect, the average county professional. This diplomatic and increasingly influential body was arguing that any profit from the tour should go back to the hard-pressed county clubs for the good of the mass of county cricketers. Their arguments prevailed, and what little extra the TCCB managed to squeeze out of the ACB during the tough negotiations between September and November was duly shared between the counties rather than the touring team, who were forced to accept that the salaries originally proposed when the matter was first raised during the final Test of the summer at the Oval were the best they could hope for.

If anyone had a serious grievance it was the Indian Board of Control and the Indian Test players. They had been due to tour Australia with England under the original scheme of the ACB, but when the agreement with PBL was made the Indians were told that West Indies would be invited in their stead. India would have to wait until 1980-81 for a slice of the rich Australian cake. They were due to tour in that year with New Zealand, followed in 1981-82 by the West Indies and Pakistan. England made it clear that in 1982-83 they expected Australia to revert to a more traditional tour format with Australia and England playing in a series of six Tests. The TCCB was obviously unaware when it released this statement that by the terms of its agreement with PBL the ACB was committed to 'arranging for the ICC to conduct a World Series Cricket Cup competed for by teams from each Test-playing country every four years, commencing no later than the fourth year of this agreement'.

But only when a more traditional tour was arranged, the TCCB declared, would the Ashes be at stake again in Australia, although in the intervening period an Ashes series in England was due in 1981. The TCCB and the administrative body at Lord's, the Cricket Council, agonised long and hard about whether to put the Ashes at stake for the short series of 1979-80. In the end, only a fortnight before the England team left and much to the chagrin of most (though certainly not all) followers of the game in Australia, George Mann, the chairman of the TCCB, phoned Bob Parish in Melbourne to announce that, for the good of the game as a whole, the Ashes would not be at stake.

The Australian Board and PBL had, not without reason, claimed a precedent. In 1974-75 Australia had regained the Ashes with a sweeping 4-1 defeat of England. Only a few months later they came to England and successfully defended the Ashes in a series of only four Tests in England. Lynton Taylor of PBL also pointed out that many of the earliest rubbers for the Ashes had been of only three Test matches, and there was talk of the Poms being 'chicken', notably in a hard-hitting and bitter speech at the Melbourne Cricket Ground by the influential Victorian cricket official Ray Steele. After all, the West Indian Board had cheerfully agreed to play for the Frank Worrell Trophy in *their* three-match series against Australia. But the Frank Worrell Trophy meant very much less than the Ashes (intrinsically, of course, an almost worthless urn containing the ashes of a bail or stump) and, in any case, this was not the point. The TCCB decision underlined their view that this was an exceptional tour, a 'one-off', made to help the Australian Board out of the difficult situation facing them in the immediate aftermath of the 'war' with WSC. Though they recognised the 1975 precedent, England pointed out that in that summer the Australians had been able to prepare fully for the Tests with a normal programme of games against the counties. This time England would have a much briefer warm-up period, and such first-class games as were planned for them outside the Tests were sometimes against moderate opposition They were travelling around a good deal and playing much more limited-over cricket than ever before, some of it under floodlights, a type of cricket of which only one member of their team – Underwood – had had experience. With no fewer than fifteen one-day internationals scheduled, plus three Tests between Australia and West Indies, the Anglo-Australian series simply could not have its normal prestige. England, in other words, were refusing to permit the cheapening of the unique Ashes tradition.

It was also true that the Australian preparation for the Tests against England would hardly be ideal. On two occasions in what turned out to be a remorselessly hectic season they were to play ten days' Test cricket in a twelve-day period. They also faced a confusion of day and night cricket and a surfeit of limited-over games. Moreover, although they now had an unprecedented number of Test players to choose from, those men who had been to India between September and November would inevitably be fairly jaded by the end of the intensive Australian season.

Before recording the course of this controversial, experimental and historically important season of Australian cricket, one should perhaps attempt a brief assessment of the immediate effects of the revolution instigated by Kerry Packer and the players who had hunted their fortunes in his employ. The happiest result of the agreement, of course, was that all players were now available for Test cricket. Moreover, by skilful and remorseless promotion of World Series Cricket, the game in Australia, *already booming before Packer's takeover* – he would not have been interested but for the boom between 1974 and 1976 – had attracted a new fringe audience of mainly young enthusiasts, the majority drawn by the novelty of cricket under lights at night. Although there was a danger of the new ideas swamping established customs which had stood the test of time, the players who had enthusiastically endorsed them had accepted the requirement to go along with some of the gimmicks and sales techniques because their own newly acquired wealth was contingent upon the continuing appeal of the game to spectators and television advertisers. It was the responsibility of the administrators to try to see the game in a broader perspective, but the players had to try to do so too. Not everything that increased their immediate wealth was necessarily good in the longer term either for themselves or for the game.

As I wrote in my account of the 1978-79 Ashes series, the overall spectator figures deny the truth of the often-quoted WSC assertion that extra spectators had been attracted to cricket; on the contrary less people watched WSC and establishment cricket put together in 1978-79 than had supported Australia in their successful series against England and the West Indies between 1974 and 1976. But there was no question that as a direct result of the Revolution all the leading players of the world were much better rewarded for getting to the top in a difficult and demanding sport. This was one beneficial result of all the rancour, and another was the attraction to cricket of even more sponsors than before. Moreover, by his refusal to sell the product cheaply, Mr Packer forced cricket administrators to realise that they could raise more from both sponsorship and television than they had done before. On the other hand it must be stressed that the new commercial approach did not guarantee financial viability for the game. Indeed World Series Cricket, whatever it might have done indirectly for the overall profits of Channel Nine and Consolidated Press (Mr Packer's parent company), had in itself resulted in a heavy financial loss. Even though it performed the function of conveniently losing some of the taxation which would have been made on the profits of other companies within the Consolidated Press group, WSC could not have been allowed to go on losing indefinitely.

The details of the financial position of the ACB and WSC were fully declared for the first time in the Board's submission recommending their agreement with PBL to the Trade Practices Commission. In the 1977-78 and 1978-79 seasons the ACB's loss was $A810,000, as mentioned above. The Board stated bluntly to the Commission that several State Associations were on the road to bankruptcy.

The Packer parent company could stand this sort of loss without any anxiety, but they reported to the Commission that Channel Nine expended a total of $A4,587,878 in their two years' coverage of WSC cricket. The advertising revenue during the cricket broadcasts was only $A1,707,430: a two-year loss of $A2,880,448 or nearly one and a half million pounds. This does not, presumably, take in many expenses (also some of the profits) involved in promoting and publicising World Series Cricket – renting grounds, paying players, etc. The overall loss to Mr Packer's companies must have been nearer £3 million.

Money, money, money! The subject had never been so freely discussed in connection with cricket as it had in the last few years. The clear danger was that this obsession with dollars and cents would lead to the price for winning becoming more important than the honour of doing so; as a result the temptations for players to indulge in gamesmanship and for fast bowlers to become bouncer-happy were greater. But golf professionals had clearly shown that bigger prizes need not necessarily amount to lesser sportsmanship. On the contrary, the bigger the stakes, the greater the need for self-control by cricketers who were now being televised and talked about from every angle. They were undoubtedly aware of this when the 1979-80 season started, and there was reason to hope that they could by a responsible attitude overcome the intense pressure upon them and so help to heal the wounds which the bitter civil war in cricket had opened.

Chapter Two

TEETHING TROUBLES

The England and West Indies teams arrived in Australia within a few hours of one another on 6 November. As if to prove that familiarity breeds contempt, and to warn the ACB that it must not in future saturate the market, the early matches were watched by very small crowds. They were not televised by Channel Nine and received no noticeable promotion from PBL. This seemed a misguided approach because the major matches in the programme surely needed less selling to the public than the minor ones.

From the players' point of view the practice matches which had been arranged were far from ideal and a good deal less competitive than the normal preparatory games against State sides at the start of an Australian tour. The West Indians played weak opposition in games at Geelong and Devonport, and England were involved in non-first-class fixtures at Newcastle and Adelaide. Curiously, they played only a three-day game against a powerful Queensland side at Brisbane but a four-day match against an inexperienced Combined Australian Universities XI at Adelaide. When the fourth day of the latter match began there were exactly eleven spectators at the Adelaide Oval as England went out to field. The whole match attracted a mere 1,476 spectators in four days.

The West Indies were the more impressive in their early games. Of the two most significant matches the West Indies beat South Australia in three days with some powerful batting and fast bowling whereas England needed the resolute batting of two of their all-rounders, Geoff Miller and Peter Willey, to eliminate the possibility of a defeat – also in three days – by Queensland. But this match was chiefly memorable for a duel between Jeff Thomson, looking as fit as he was determined, and England's experimental opening pair, Derek Randall and Geoff Boycott. The latter looked in altogether better form than he had at any stage of his disappointing tour the previous year, and though he was out for 11 and 20, both times to the left-arm over-the-wicket Schuller, he appeared to be in calm control of Thomson. Randall, in contrast, was brilliant one moment, vulnerable the next. He made a sparkling 97, hitting 14 boundaries, on the first day, but was out to a poor stroke against Thomson on the second, moving towards his leg-stump and snicking a rapid delivery to the bearded Greg Chappell at first slip.

As it happened, this was the only wicket which Thomson managed to take in the match, although there was little life in the Brisbane pitch for him to exploit. In this spell in particular, on the second evening of the match, he bowled some very fast deliveries, but he was not quite the terrifying prospect he had been four years before. Only time would tell how he would fare when he resumed his partnership with Dennis Lillee, with Rodney Hogg, England's tormentor the year before, in support.

Soon after the announcement of the ACB/PBL agreement Lillee had said that he would be 'pretty dirty' if he was not selected to play for Australia again in normal circumstances. Despite lacking some of his old fire in the early Sheffield Shield games, he was duly chosen in an Australian twelve for the first Test and first one-day international as part of a four-pronged fast attack comprising also Thomson, Hogg and Geoff Dymock, the sturdy Queenslander who had been one of the few successes of the Australian tour of India between September and November under the captaincy of Kim Hughes. Thomson had to withdraw from the international because of a sprained ankle and was replaced by Len Pascoe. Amongst other candidates for the seam bowling places in the Australian team were Mick Malone, Max Walker, Gary Gilmour and two uncapped prospects, Geoff Lawson of New South Wales and Terry Alderman of West Australia.

Competition for places in the Australian side had never been keener, if only because there were some forty players with Test experience in contention. This, of course, was the result of the schism, which had presented several promising young cricketers with a chance at the highest level which they would not have earned so soon in normal times. After the one-five defeat against England and another in the first of two Test matches against Pakistan Graham Yallop had lost his position as national captain to Kim Hughes, who managed to reverse the tide of defeat at Perth in the second Test against Pakistan. He was less successful in the Prudential World Cup in England in June, Australia winning only against Canada, and on the tour of India Australia lost a rubber (2-0) to India for the first time. Hughes, however, arrived home from the wearying tour in November with his reputation enhanced, both as a capable and personable captain and as a batsman of high class. He scored 592 runs in the six Tests at an average of just under 60. Graham Yallop, who hit a fine 167 as an opening batsman at Calcutta; Allan Border, who made 521 Test runs at 43.42, including a hundred at Madras in the first Test; and Dymock, with 24 wickets at 24.17, were the other Australian successes. By contrast Hogg was a conspicuous failure after his dramatic introduction to Test cricket a few months before (41 wickets in the series against England and 10 more in two Tests against Pakistan). He took only 11 wickets in the six Tests against India at an average of 53 each and once or twice produced a petulant outburst which did not endear him to the Indian public. But as soon as he returned to Australia he started to bowl well again, and six wickets for South Australia in the first innings of the match against the West Indies assured him of a place in the Australian team.

The batting places were as toughly contested as the fast-bowling ones. Laird and McCosker were the two opening batsmen eventually chosen. Laird, the small fair-haired West Australian right-hander, had toured England in 1975 without gaining a Test place but had enhanced his reputation in two years with WSC. Other openers in the running for places included Ian Davis, Andy Hilditch, Rick Darling, Graeme Wood and the uncapped Victorian Julian Wiener. The middle-order batsmen chosen for Australia's first two matches were Border, Greg Chappell, Hughes and David Hookes, the left-handed South Australian who had been one of WSC's greatest attractions. Greg Chappell was made captain, with Hughes as his deputy, Ian Chappell having effectively disqualified himself by abusing players and an umpire in a Sheffield Shield match for South Australia against Tasmania, thus earning a three-week suspension. Yallop, Peter Toohey, the uncapped Martin Kent (a WSC success) and the veterans Ross Edwards and Doug Walters were other batsmen with hopes of forcing their way into the side before the long season was over.

It was widely expected that fast bowlers would dominate the scene, and the Australian selection panel, this year comprising Phil Ridings (Chairman) from South Australia, Sam Loxton from Victoria, Alan Davidson from New South Wales, and Ray Lindwall from Queensland, plus the reigning Australian captain (Hughes for the first Test, Greg Chappell for the remainder) chose only one spinner for the first two games. The leg-spinning incumbent Jim Higgs had had a disappointing tour of India, so it was no surprise when the stocky Victorian left-arm orthodox bowler Ray Bright was preferred to him. Bright had the advantage of being a much better batsman and fielder. Ashley Mallett had also emerged from retirement to challenge for a place. Two other spinners had played Tests in India, namely Bruce Yardley and Peter Sleep.

There was never much doubt that one of the national idols, Rodney Marsh, would resume his duties behind the stumps, although his reappearance after two years as one of the widely publicised front-men of the WSC set-up was a heavy blow to the promising young wicket-keeper Kevin Wright, who had replaced him in the West Australian and Australian teams. Wright plummeted from Test to Grade A cricket like a winged grouse. Much money, as well as prestige, was lost to players like Wright and Graeme Wood, neither of whom was able to find a State place on their return from India.

The English and West Indian teams were more easily chosen, although England's selectors had needed seven hours to make up their minds when meeting in London in September. The most contentious decision was not so much the recall of Derek Underwood after two years with WSC (had he stayed in Test cricket he must have come close to the Test bowling record) as the omission of Philippe Edmonds. Only a week before the team was announced Edmonds had been freely discussed as a possible successor to Mike Brearley as England (and Middlesex) captain. Edmonds felt that Brearley had been against his inclusion in the touring party. 'Knowing how persuasive Mike can be,' he said, 'I am not really surprised.' Geoff Boycott, on the other hand, was. When told that Edmonds had been left out of the party of sixteen he said: 'I am absolutely staggered. Derek is a unique bowler and I would have had them both, but Phil is not far short of Derek as a bowler and is a better batsman and fielder.'

Gifted all-round cricketer though Edmonds is, it had to be admitted that his recent form bore no comparison with that of Underwood, who had taken more than 100 wickets in an outstanding season for Kent and whose expertise in limited-over cricket, which was to be such an important feature of the tour, was well known. Moreover his record in Australia was a good one, whereas Edmonds had been disappointing on tour the previous year, playing only in the first Test match. On this evidence John Emburey, later to join the team as a replacement, was at least as unfortunate. Emburey was bracketed with Pat Pocock by fellow-professionals in English county cricket as the best off-spin bowler in the country. He had certainly bowled beautifully in Australia the year before, taking 16 Test wickets at 19.13. But on the previous tour there had been six Tests instead of three: now the emphasis would inevitably be on faster bowlers and, given the essential inclusion of Underwood as perhaps the world's most feared slow bowler, the other spinners chosen had to be able to bat too.

The selectors decided that two off-spinners would be more likely to succeed in Australia than two left-arm orthodox spinners, and Peter Willey of Northamptonshire took over Emburey's place as partner, or rival, for the established Geoff Miller, who was a certainty after his 23 wickets against Australia on the last tour. Willey had made sure of his place by a splendid all-round performance in the final Test of the English summer against India, when he made 52 and 31 and took 2 for 96 in 43.5 overs, proving his ability to keep free-scoring batsmen at heel by bowling very steadily during an exciting helter-skelter for runs by India on the last day.

Chris Old, Roger Tolchard and Clive Radley were the three other members of the 1978-79 team missing from this one. Old had had a busy benefit year with Yorkshire and medical advisers told him that a tough tour would not improve his chances of giving Yorkshire further prolonged service. He had so frequently been unfit to play for England that his achievements in Test cricket hadn't done justice to his vast natural talents; on the other hand, whenever he had taken the field for England in one piece he had always given one hundred percent, and although often failing with the bat he never did so with the ball except when he was overwhelmed by the West

Indian batsmen in the Caribbean in 1973-74. His fielding too had been brilliant, either in the slips or in the deep.

Old's place went to a 20-year-old bowler from Kent who had played only one full season of first-class cricket, Graham Dilley. A strapping six-foot three-inch blond-haired fast-medium bowler who had improved with every game and who already possessed the potential to become really fast, Dilley had dedicated himself to cricket after leaving his teenage job as a diamond-setter at Hatton Garden (in fact he was sacked after going off to play for Kent Second XI). He was soon to justify his selection despite some talk early in the tour that his action was suspect. The former Test umpire Lou Rowan told me in Queensland that, as far as he was concerned, it was 'pure as the driven snow'. The story quickly died.

Various other alternatives had been in the selectors' notebooks during the season. Willie Hogg of Lancashire bowled quite well for MCC against the Indian touring team at Lord's in an unofficial Test trial, and Les Taylor of Leicestershire, a strongly built former coalminer with an ungainly action but distinct pace off the pitch, also had his supporters. Both these two ruled themselves out by breaking down before the season was over. Of two younger prospects Hugh Wilson of Surrey was promising but clearly not quite ready, and Jonathan Agnew of Leicestershire had not been able to build up the physique to go with his naturally good action and definite speed. The official reserve, therefore, became the Yorkshire all-rounder Graham Stevenson who had for several years been considered one of England's more hopeful fast-bowling prospects because of his strength and excellent action. He had, in fact, been to Australia in 1976-77 on a Whitbread scholarship, faring rather better than Ian Botham in Melbourne Grade cricket, although Botham, of course, was soon to leave him and all other young all-rounders in England far behind. Stevenson took 8 for 75 against Lancashire in 1978 to earn his county cap with a performance of real hostility, and thereafter he was in the minds of the selectors, who would perhaps have called upon him sooner had he shown more consistency. As it was, having narrowly missed selection for the tour after taking 46 Championship wickets for Yorkshire in 1979 at an average of 29.65 (Dilley had taken 46 at 23.82), Stevenson was sent for towards the end of November when

Mike Hendrick showed signs of making only a very slow recovery from a shoulder injury and when it was also clear that Bob Willis was going to struggle to last the stern course which lay ahead.

Hendrick and Willis, with Botham as their main support and Lever and Old in reserve, had done much to win the series in Australia the previous winter. But Willis was seldom a happy-looking bowler on the field, suffering early in the tour from severely blistered feet and later from a serious loss of rhythm in his far from classical action. His own guts, and the unwavering faith in him shown by his colleagues, enabled him to take 20 wickets in the Tests at 23.05, 13 of these coming in the first two matches at Brisbane and Perth. But in the four Cornhill Tests against India in the British summer Willis took only 10 wickets at 29.80, often looking lacklustre though he was trying as hard as ever. He took only nine wickets in eight first-class games for Warwickshire at a cost of 42 runs each. This was nothing short of embarrassing for the country's leading fast bowler, but such was Willis's influence for good on the England team that the selectors had no hesitation in again making him Brearley's deputy.

Mike Hendrick's part in retaining the Ashes had been an even bigger one. In his own right he had taken 19 wickets in the five Tests in which he played at only 15 runs each, and by his phenomenal accuracy and the extra bounce he achieved on Australian pitches he had harried the young Australian batsmen so mercilessly that they often got themselves out at the other end. Against India he took 12 more wickets at 18 runs each until, on the final morning of the series, he had to leave the field with a painful shoulder injury, the legacy of a dive to take a catch earlier in the season when he had landed heavily on his all-important right shoulder. He was worried that the damage might be more or less permanent and although, having rested the shoulder, he suffered no pain in training before the tour began, when he bowled against Queensland in the opening match of the tour more sharp pain drove him off the field again. After a fortnight of great anxiety for a man desperately hoping for a successful tour at the start of his benefit year with Derbyshire, Hendrick was unable to bowl at full pace in the nets at Adelaide and a specialist reported that the injury might recur at any time under physical stress. It was a cruel blow to

Hendrick only a year after establishing himself as an integral member of the England side and an equally great blow to England's chances in their current campaign. Not only in the Tests, but also in the limited-over matches where his accuracy was so valuable, Hendrick had been a key part of Brearley's strategy. His injury, however, gave John Lever the chance to establish himself anew after a highly successful season of county cricket for Essex during which he had taken more than 100 wickets for the second year running and helped his county – indeed often inspired them – to their first Championship title.

If England's fast-bowling position was in a state of flux at the start of the tour – and hardly to be compared in terms of speed and hostility with the West Indian and Australian attacks – Brearley did at least have at his side the incomparable talent of Ian Botham, who earlier in the year had reached 1000 Test runs and 100 Test wickets in 21 Tests, less than any other player, and he also had a better balanced attack with Underwood, Miller and Willey able to exploit any dusty pitches which might be encountered.

As with so many England sides of recent vintage, however, a serious doubt existed about England's ability to score enough runs for their accurate bowlers and usually brilliant fielders to work upon. Brearley himself had been an automatic choice as captain for what, he stated clearly before his departure, would be his final overseas tour. Although one had given up hope that he would fully justify his presence in the side as a batsman alone, he clearly had a better chance than any other possible England captain of outwitting Clive Lloyd and Greg Chappell. His shrewd, unflappable and sympathetic leadership more than counterbalanced his lack of runs. There was a negative reason, also, for sticking with Brearley, for if England's recent successful run were destined to come to an end against the formidable opposition now awaiting them after two relatively easy years during the period of upheaval in world cricket caused by the Packer Revolution, it was far better that Brearley should be the suffering captain rather than some unfortunate successor who would have the task of rebuilding after he had gone. The confidence of any successor named at this stage might not have survived the possible defeats ahead.

Had Brearley himself been a lesser man with an eye to the

judgement of history, he would probably have resigned the captaincy before the tour began, considering how heavily all the bookmakers were stacking the odds against him. But all those cricket writers who suggested that he was 'making one tour too many' seemed to miss the point. In the wider interest of English cricket Brearley was more expendable than a younger man: also he was not someone whose life depended upon cricketing success. His ability as a captain, and the good fortune he had had to be in the right place at the right time, had made him much richer in a material sense than he could ever have hoped five years before, but much of the rest of his life would be spent outside cricket's magic circle and he already had plans firmly laid for a longer-term career in psychoanalysis.

After another disappointing season with the bat for England Brearley was no longer considered to be a serious proposition as an opening batsman at Test level. Geoff Boycott, however, certainly still was after rebounding from a traumatic tour of Australia the previous year to average 102.53 from a mere 20 first-class innings in the English season. Incidentally Alan Butcher, who won his first Test cap as Boycott's opening partner in the last Test at the Oval, played 42 innings in the season, underlining how, especially in a World Cup year, England players tend to get far less match practice than county players. Butcher did not impress enough to get the vacant opener's spot for the tour, which instead went to Wayne Larkins, a gifted strokeplayer who had played for England in the Prudential World Cup but had yet to play a Test.

Clive Radley, though he was as reliable as ever for Middlesex, had dropped out of contention at the highest level after his failure in Australia, and the other batting places went to David Gower, Graham Gooch and Derek Randall – all brilliant strokeplayers prone to inconsistency. Upon their ability to withstand the fierce pace and hostility of the West Indian and Australian fast bowlers depended England's chances of making a success of the tour. Places for these three had not been in doubt: although Randall had lost his place for the last Test of the summer his form in Australia on two visits made him a certainty even before he finished off his season for Nottinghamshire by making 209 and 146 *as an opening batsman* against Middlesex at Trent Bridge. This encouraged England to experiment with Randall as an opener at the start of the tour.

England's players knew each other well, were used to success, and at least began the tour as a fit, disciplined, well-balanced and well-organised team. Whether, if they held their chances in the field, these factors would cancel out their relative lack of fire-power, everyone would soon know.

Very few doubts troubled West Indian supporters. Both in WSC cricket and in winning the World Cup in 1975 and 1979 they had proved themselves the best side of limited-over cricketers in the world. But their Test record in Australia was unbelievably bad. They had never defeated Australia away from home and in 1975-76 Clive Lloyd's team had suffered a humiliating five-one defeat against Greg Chappell's. Though Lloyd himself was now a veteran, and his leading fast bowler at that time, Andy Roberts, was also nearing the end of his career, other young players had grown up considerably since that tour and Lloyd now presided over a team of such abundant natural ability that they started the jamboree of internationals and Tests with the best chance of picking up most of the prizes.

At the start of the season six of the seven specialist batsmen in the West Indian squad of 16 players – Lloyd, Alvin Kallicharran, Viv Richards, Desmond Haynes, Gordon Greenidge, and Lawrence Rowe – averaged between 43 and 60 in Test cricket. Larry Gomes, the other batsman, averaged 35 and already had two Test centuries to his credit. For England only Gower and Boycott averaged over 40, and whereas the West Indian side had amassed 43 Test centuries between them England could boast only 27, of which Boycott had made 18. But England had beaten Australia in Australia many times: the West Indies never had. It would be fascinating to see if this time they could lay the bogey.

Only in the slow-bowling department were they weak. Derek Parry, the off-spinner from Nevis, was the only specialist spinner in the side. But the wicket-keeping was in safe hands – Deryck Murray with David Murray in reserve – and the fast-bowling quintet of Roberts, Holding, Garner, Croft and Marshall, with Collis King as a supporting all-rounder, was a terrifying enough prospect for batsmen.

One of the many interesting possibilities before the matches began was that far from becoming a bouncer war the games between West Indies and Australia might actually be relatively bouncer-free because the battery of fast bowlers on each side might have a deterrent effect on one another. Lillee and Thomson, who had come out on top in 1975-76, were no longer such a formidable combination, whereas West Indies, however much Roberts might be a fading star, had Holding at his best supported by the mountainous Garner, who was now perhaps the most difficult bowler in the world to play on a pitch with any life in it.

The pitches were sure to have an important effect on the way the game was played: it was essential for cricket as a spectacle that batsmen should have more of a chance against the fast bowlers than they had had the previous season. The umpires, too, had a vital role to play. Their decisions would come under scrutiny as never before because of the sheer extent of Channel Nine's coverage and its ability to show a given incident from almost any angle. It was essential that the umpires should exercise firm control and a calm, fair and consistent interpretation of the laws.

However apathetic the Australian public may have been towards the warm-up matches played by England and the West Indies, there was no doubt about the early interest in the big matches. As one awaited with mixed feelings the first of the fifteen limited-over internationals and six Test matches which lay ahead one could almost hear the chorus of young Australian voices raised as one: 'C'mon Aussie, C'mon, C'mon, C'mon Aussie C'mon.'

We were all in Sydney now, the novel programme was about to start and, at least for the moment, there was no turning-back for anyone.

Chapter Three

DISAPPOINTMENTS FOR WEST INDIES

Tuesday 27 November 1979. A beautiful day in Sydney. Temperature 23 degrees Centigrade. A stiff breeze and much less humid than it often is at Sydney in early summer. The cricket ground is about one-third filled with spectators when the first international between Australia and West Indies, one of fifteen due in the next ten weeks to decide the Benson and Hedges World Series Cup, begins at ten minutes past two. The ground will fill steadily during the sunny afternoon, reaching a total of 21,168 by the time that the lights come on. By half-past five the last specks of green have disappeared from the Hill, which is a mass of bodies. More than half are young men stripped to the waist, soaking in the sun, 'eskies' at their side. Yet the well-spaced seats in front of the old Edwardian pavilion on the other side of the ground are almost entirely empty. The masses seem to want this sort of cricket, the members apparently don't. At the height of the match, though, the ground is three-quarters full, suggesting that last year's WSC figures were 'exaggerated'.

The first appearance of the players offends the eye of the seasoned cricket watcher. The umpires are dressed in black crew-neck body-shirts with black trousers; with their white hats they look like fully paid-up members of the Mafia: only the cigars are missing. The Australians are in what appear to be white track-suits with gold and green stripes down the side of shoulders and legs. When the West Indies openers, Greenidge and Haynes, emerge from the dignified old pavilion they look out of place on a cricket ground, straight out of a baseball match. Haynes's helmet is red, Greenidge's maroon. Both have maroon pads and broad maroon stripes across the shoulders. It takes time to forget the clothes and to concentrate on the game. But soon the cricket itself compels attention.

Chappell's decision to put the West Indies in to bat is surprising. This very same West Indies eleven was put in to bat by Brearley at Lord's in June, got into trouble, escaped and went on to win the Prudential World Cup. Moreover the pitch looks bland, and it would seem preferable to bat with the sun burning in mid-afternoon than with the dew rising after supper. Still, Chappell knows what he is doing. Perhaps he thinks the tension will get the West Indian batsmen out.

Lillee and Pascoe open the bowling with the new white ball. Pascoe has come into the side as replacement for his old surfing mate Jeff Thomson, who is nursing a sprained ankle in Brisbane but expects to be fit for the Test match. Hogg was picked before Pascoe but he does not get the new ball. Hogg is not of the WSC magic circle, and Chappell knows Pascoe better. He bowls well too, fast, straight and to a full length, but it is Lillee, also eschewing the bouncer, who gets the early wickets. Greenidge drives over a searing, swinging half-volley and loses his middle stump; Richards tries to hook a ball that isn't short enough and is l.b.w.: 18 for two in the seventh over.

Kallicharran, supposedly out of touch until his hundred in the last game at Devonport, plays well from the start: neat, cool, hitting the ball off the middle of the bat with a rich, mellow ring. Haynes plays sensibly too for a while. Lillee comes off after taking two for ten in six overs, Pascoe after five overs: no wicket for 14. Hogg replaces Lillee at the Noble Stand end; Bright, preferred to Dymock in the Australian eleven, relieves Pascoe at the Randwick end. Kallicharran doesn't mind Bright, who goes for 26 in five overs. What does Dymock think, carrying out the drinks now after taking 24 wickets in the Indian heat?

Haynes gets reckless. He hooks at Hogg, is beaten for pace and the ball lobs towards the bowler in a gentle parabola. A girl of seven could catch it, but Hogg's legs turn to jelly and he drops it. The colour drains from his face. Chappell puts his head in his hands. Marsh says what Marsh usually says. The crowd tells Hogg what it thinks of him – and his parents – but such is the bedlam that the comment of any one barracker cannot be heard any more. Gone, long and irrevocably, are the days of Yabba and other wits on the Hill: now it is just the mindless chanting of the mob. An over later Haynes again skies Hogg and gets away with it as the ball plops into no-man's-land.

Border, the gentle reserve spinner, takes over from Bright, the established one. He soon bowls Haynes for 29. Lloyd lopes out, looking relaxed and determined to enjoy himself. There is an interval at ten past four, after 28 overs. No one is quite sure when the interval is due, but we learn later that it comes at four o'clock unless 28 overs have not been bowled, in which case that number must be completed before refreshments are due. During the interval Lloyd is interviewed by one of Channel Nine's yellow-blazered army of commentators. Fred Trueman is one of them – he has just won an award as radio sports personality of the year in Britain. Times have certainly changed: fancy interviewing a batsman in the middle of an important innings! But we must not forget: this match is being promoted largely for a television audience.

It is interesting how often intervals are followed by the fall of a wicket: two in this case. Both the left-handers, first Kalli for 49, then Lloyd for 16, fall to Border. At this point he has taken three for 21 in six overs. So much for ferocious fast bowlers and the bouncer war!

King and Murray pull the innings round. King plays not as well as in his brilliant, flaying innings at Lord's in June, but he again hits the ball very hard and with no inhibitions. Murray also looks in good nick. He too got a century in Devonport.

The return of Pascoe brings the West Indies to heel again, though Hogg rather than Lillee gets the honour of bowling the last few overs at the other end. Is this a sign of sensitive, long-term captaincy by Chappell, or has Lillee got to be carefully preserved, like the best china for the best dinner-parties?

Pascoe bowls very well again: just as before he delivers fast and to a full length. The batsmen swing and miss; he hits. He bowls King for 29, Murray for 27 and Roberts for 16. Garner is the victim of the inevitable late-innings limited-over run-out. Pascoe finishes with four for 29, Hogg with none for 49: but the latter's place is assured for the first Test at least, and he has had no luck.

The 'dinner-break' is distinctly unpleasant. The journalists are displeased that while Channel Nine producers, publicity people and associated pretty girls quaff wine and turkey, not even a meat pie is available in the deserted press-room. Not that it worries me. I am trying to telephone reports to the BBC on the telephone and I simply cannot hear a word above the deafening music echoing from the loud-speakers off the aluminium roof. No one is surprised by the first tune they play: 'C'mon, Aussie, C'mon.' The lyrics are new ones, written especially for 1979-80: one for Australia, one for West Indies, one for England. The poet laureate who wrote them seems pretty sure that Australia will tan the hide – that's his expression – off all-comers. He could be right, but somehow the jingoism makes one hope he is not. Between the songs the PBL man on the public address system has a great deal of trouble convincing the youths who are cavorting on the outfield that two sky-divers are due at any moment and will cause an accident if the ground is not cleared. Down they come eventually. But we have seen it all before, not to mention the majorettes, who provide the second part of the interval entertainment.

Again it takes time to adjust to the serious business of cricket. Australia's innings starts in the difficult twilight hour, when the lights wrestle for prominence with the fading sun. Gradually voltage power rules as the sky turns orange, then deep pink, blue and finally pitch black against the yellow-white square of light which shines like a mighty halo over the SCG.

McCosker is beaten for pace and l.b.w. to Holding in the second over, but Laird plays neatly off his legs and Border quite well too, although appearing to be uncertain whether to play himself in as in a normal match or to go for his shots. Both fall to Croft and Australia are only 52 for three when Hughes, vice-captain, joins Chappell. The captain has already survived a jubilant appeal for a catch behind by Murray, to the second ball he faced from Croft. But he has straight-driven the next for four to show what he thinks of the appeal – and of the publicly displayed disapproval by the West Indians when the umpire says 'not out'.

Hughes looks brimful of confidence, hitting the ball into the gaps both hard and stylishly. The West Indies are in trouble, partly because King has not come onto the field because of a severe sinus complaint and Richards is having to be used as the fifth bowler. He bowls tight off-spinners successfully enough until Hughes suddenly dances gymnastically down the pitch and carts him far up into the seething masses on the Hill. Their ecstasy is complete. The white ball rising high into the black night sky makes a dramatic sight. Australia will win now for sure. Chappell survives a vehement appeal for l.b.w. by Richards when he is 37. Hughes gets to 50 first, then is bowled off his pads by Richards.

Hookes, made into a pin-up boy by the PBL publicity men, gets a hero's welcome from the Hill, then sweeps and misses at Richards's second ball and walks back again disconsolately. Has he grown up yet? Certainly not as much as Hughes, who missed all the WSC promotion and was probably lucky to do so. Still, Hookes has time yet to erase the impression he gave in England in 1977 of a brilliantly gifted but immature batsman, a frisky colt yet to be schooled to tackle the big fences.

Marsh has long ago learned to restrain his impetuosity. He takes the ones and twos that are on offer now the field is spread. Lloyd keeps calm, but he can do nothing unless he gets Chappell out, and Chappell is in firm control. He hooks the winning four off the first ball of the 49th over. Victory for Australia by five wickets.

Soon afterwards the door of the West Indian dressing-room is kicked off its hinges by a person or persons unknown. The West Indian camp denies responsibility, but admits to being very upset about two decisions given in Chappell's favour. So it ends on a sour note after all, though not for Chappell, who collects a team cheque of $A3,000 and a man of the match award of $500 (£1,500 and £250 respectively).

*   *   *

For much of its course England's opening international against the West Indies the following day and night was an altogether less frenzied occasion. But the match finally exploded into a most dramatic finale. The crowd was smaller: at first very small indeed but soon growing on a cool, cloudy day to 6,120. Lloyd won the toss and put England in on a pitch as dead and true as the one the day before. The West Indians looked subdued, and their fielding was poor, their bowling indifferent as England built on an opening partnership of 79 between Randall and Brearley to total 211 for eight in their 50 overs, a rate of 4.22 runs per over.

England, mindful of the mistakes they had made in the Prudential Cup Final, had left Boycott out of their eleven – the first time he had ever been excluded during a tour when available for a major representative match. Brearley therefore took on the opener's role again and did an admirable job as second fiddle to Randall, who played excellently. Brearley decided after eighteen relatively friendly overs that the time had come for him to get on or get out, and he straight-drove Parry and clipped Croft off his legs for well-timed fours before chipping Parry's off-spin to Greenidge to depart for 25 in the 23rd over.

Randall well deserved a fifty but fell to an indecisive shot one short of that score, and Gooch, also in two minds, gave Parry a return catch soon afterwards, so England were unable to keep the momentum going and, for a time, Gower and Willey had to consolidate at no more than three runs an over. But with Gower taking the leading role these two almost doubled that rate for a time, exposing some shoddy West Indian ground fielding and the lack of venom in their attack on a placid pitch.

It is interesting how reputations can vary from one country to another. Joel Garner, who had bowled so well in England both for Somerset and in the Prudential Cup for his country, was accorded greater respect by England than he had been the day before by Australia; Croft, on the other hand, had been relatively unsuccessful in county cricket, and despite his excellent record in the West Indies, and in Australia, English batsmen were less worried by his height and sway-away inswing action. Eventually they all came alike to Peter Willey, who took on the lead part when Gower had been bowled by Croft for 44 and finished with 58 not out off 65 balls. England's total might have been higher had Botham, on this occasion, used a bit more brain and a bit less brawn.

Botham, however, had been promoted to membership of the tour selection committee, a clear indication that he was a possible future captain. It can be no coincidence that since Brearley became captain, the England selectors had been a good deal more flexible than in the Illingworth/Greig era. At least Brearley was prepared to learn from his mistakes. Thus Boycott and Taylor were at this stage kept for the less frantic demands of Test cricket, and places were found for Willey and Bairstow. Thus also Graham Dilley was not only selected for England in a major representative match for the first time at the age of 20 but he was also given the new ball ahead of Bob

Willis, who can only narrowly have been preferred to John Lever. Again, England had lost their limited-over series to Australia the previous winter partly because they had played five fast bowlers in one match at Melbourne on a lifeless wicket. This time Brearley used three seamers and three spinners.

They all served him well, but it developed into a desperate affair. At first England seemed well in control as Dilley sent down four very fast overs and might have had Haynes out twice and Greenidge once before Haynes eventually played a wild shot and was bowled. Greenidge, however, hobbling on a bad ankle one moment, sprinting quick singles the next, survived hard chances to Brearley and Randall and drove both Dilley and Botham for successive fours. When Underwood replaced Botham, the limp miraculously disappeared again as Greenidge leapt out like a pouncing cat to savage the ball high over long-off for six.

At the other end Rowe, replacing Richards who had a worrying hip injury, played in his usual cool manner, hitting the ball skilfully through mid-wicket. West Indies had reached 68 for one when Greenidge miscued a drive at Miller's curling off-spin and fell for 42 (six fours and a six).

Kallicharran and Rowe started another useful partnership and the game was only slightly in England's favour when a shower blew across the SCG and held up play for twenty minutes. It had been agreed between all parties that each of these international matches would have an adjudicator to decide what to do in the event of rain, because the Sydney City Council had ruled that the floodlights must be extinguished at half-past ten at the latest. Fred Bennett of the ACB, entrusted with the referee's job on this occasion, ruled that the West Indies innings should be reduced to 47 overs and their target proportionately reduced according to the run-rate which they had required at the start of their innings, namely 4.23. They had already slipped behind this rate before the shower and in the hectic hour of cricket which followed, despite a determined innings by Kallicharran, they never succeeded in lowering the rate below five an over. On the other hand, with wickets in hand they could afford to take chances, and the excitement grew more tense.

The new West Indian target after the shower was 199 from

47 overs. Willis came on for the first time as late as the 33rd over, held back by Brearley partly because he had wanted to let Dilley loose early, partly because he knew Willis would be useful at the height of the storm, and partly because he hoped that a dew might come down at this time to freshen up the dead pitch. It did not do so, however, nor did the shower seem to have an effect. (The pitch had quickly been covered.)

This was a critical match for Willis. He had begun the tour unimpressively and if he bowled badly now England would probably lose. He conceded eight runs in his first over to Kallicharran, but thereafter bowled an excellent line and length whilst the calm and sturdy Willey bowled his tight off-spin to even greater effect at the members' end, conceding 29 runs in eight overs. Miller – one for 33 in 10 overs – had been equally effective.

After Willey, Brearley had all the experience of Underwood to turn to, and as the strokes began to get more reckless the wickets started to fall. At 132, in the 35th over, Rowe was hit on the pads by a ball from Willis, tried to take a leg-bye, was sent back but turned too late because the acrobatic Randall was leaping at the stumps to remove the bails – unnecessarily so as it transpired because the umpire had lifted his finger at the other end to signal l.b.w.

At 143 Lloyd, batting with a runner because of his knee injury, lofted Willis into Brearley's safe hands. An over later, the 38th, Murray miscued Underwood to Gower at mid-wicket, and at 155 Parry was bowled by Underwood for 4. Kalli was still there, picking up runs off most deliveries he received, but the position looked hopeless for the West Indies until Roberts began to lay about him. For Underwood to be hit for six once is rare; twice in one evening almost defied belief but Roberts achieved it with a swirling drive over long-off into the Bradman Stand. Then, at 177 for six in the 44th over, with the tide turning fast, Roberts chipped a ball from Underwood over Randall's head at mid-wicket. With phenomenal speed Randall sprinted back, leapt upwards and backwards, and held the ball at the full extent of his right arm.

Another brilliant bit of fielding decided the game in the 45th over when Kallicharran, eighth out at 185, was beaten by a throw at close range from Gooch, who had only one stump to aim at. Holding lofted Underwood to Gower at long-on, but even then, with Brearley setting his field deep, the massive Garner, by placing the ball for ones and twos, succeeded in turning a target of ten off the last over into only three runs required from the final ball. Much to the indignation of many observers even Bairstow the wicket-keeper peeled off his gloves and went down to deep long-stop as Botham, entrusted by Brearley with the final over and keeping the ball to a full length, ran in to bowl to Croft. In a confused flurry of pads and bat the ball just scraped Croft's leg-stump and England were the winners by two runs – or perhaps more strictly on a faster scoring rate.

It was limited-over cup-tie cricket at its most exciting, a relative novelty to Australian spectators although the English players and most of their West Indian opponents knew this sort of contest well from county cricket.

For England it had been a memorable start; for the West Indies, though they had done well to get so close in the end and though their injured players gave them a legitimate excuse for failure, the first two matches had been one long day/nightmare. As for the promoters, they could be well satisfied by the impact the matches had made but less so with the behaviour of the crowds who on both nights had given the police a great deal of work. There were numerous fights; oranges and cans were thrown onto the outfield; and people relieved themselves on the covers after the first game (which also saw the incident of the dressing-room door and a West Indian player pushing an over-excited spectator to the ground).

After the second match one of the umpires, Arthur Watson, was overpowered, knocked over and stunned by the crowd rushing onto the field at the end. This sort of thing needed to be quickly nipped in the bud by joint action from the police and the ACB. Channel Nine decided not to allow journalists access to scenes of violence on videotape.

While England journeyed south in good heart to the relatively peaceful backwater of Hobart, the Australians and West Indians went north to the heat and humidity of Brisbane for what most of the true aficionados of Australian cricket still believed to be the 'real thing': a five-day Test.

The West Indians were facing a critical test of their resilience. Clive Lloyd stayed behind in Sydney for an exploratory operation on his injured knee and, after a few chips of bone had been removed, hope was expressed that he would be back within a fortnight. For a time, however, Deryck Murray was in charge and in sweltering heat on 1 December it was he who won the toss in front of the television cameras. The toss in a Test match used to be a private affair. This one must have taken some twenty minutes in all, with the captains having to wait for the coin to arrive by parachutist. As the correspondent of *The Times* remarked, it would not be long before the bottom of the scorecard in *Wisden* would record not only the umpires but also the parachutists!

After the long wait Murray chose to put Australia in on a pitch looking very different from the one on which Australia had collapsed against England a year before. Such grass as had been left by the curator, Jack Macandrew, was bleached white. The weather had been kind to him for once during the preparatory period and he knew that this time the batsmen would have a fair chance.

It did not take long for the pitch to be confirmed as a beauty, with a bit of bounce, but true bounce, and just enough pace for anything of poor length to whistle off the bat. The West Indies had Richards back in the side, although he was still concerned about his injured hip, and instead of looking for some variety in their attack by including the off-spin of Parry they plumped for the four big fast bowlers, Holding, Roberts, Garner and Croft. Australia's policy was different. Dymock was made their twelfth man for the umpteenth time, Thomson for Pascoe being the only change.

Whatever one thought of the preliminaries, the Gabba as usual was a spectacular setting for the Test. The handsome modern stands were set off by a vivid splash of orange, the abundant blossom of the poinciana trees which flower in Brisbane in December.

There was some early swing for Roberts and Holding but the colour of the pitch was almost white and it was not until the second wave of West Indian fast bowlers swept in that McCosker and Laird, the opening pair, appeared to have any difficulty. McCosker was out to Croft's first delivery, unwisely hooking before he had given himself a chance to judge the pace and bounce of the new bowler and top-edging a gentle catch to Kallicharran running back at slip.

Border looked a little afraid to assert himself now that he was a prime choice for the full Australian eleven, WSC men and all. With Garner and Croft maintaining a line he took 21 minutes to get his first run and then edged a good delivery, which lifted and left him, to the wicket-keeper.

At the end of the first hour Australia were 28 for two. A bagpipe band began practising noisily for their lunchtime performance: it was not clear whether they were trying to encourage Laird (of Scottish descent) or whether they were playing a lament for McCosker. In any case Laird, in his first Test innings, was already laying the solid foundations of a praiseworthy innings. Early on he was twice rapped on the right hand by mean, lifting deliveries. A pain-killing spray was applied to a severe bruise on the thumb; but one had the impression that Laird would have gritted it out, pain-killers or not. His technique was soundness itself, most of his strokes being played into the 'V' between mid-off and mid-on, his feet always behind the line of the ball.

Chappell, now wearing the increasingly fashionable beard (not so bushy as Mike Brearley's black mass which had been the delight of cartoonists from the moment he first put it on public display), looked good from the start. He was off the mark with a square-cut for four off Garner and only Holding had him in any difficulty early in his innings, shooting one through his defence outside the off-stump and inducing a four off the edge through the slips. But Chappell was quick to punish anything short or overpitched, hooking and cutting Roberts for two boundaries in three balls.

Chappell and Laird added 50 at almost a run a minute, 27 off Chappell's bat, but when the captain was 29 not out, just before lunch, the West Indies missed the chance to nip in the bud the most productive partnership of the innings. Chappell checked an intended straight drive to a slower ball from Roberts who could not hold on to the return catch in front of his face.

The sultry afternoon must have seemed to the West Indians to stretch ahead like a long, hard road to bare-footed pedestrians as the runs began to flow freely again after lunch. It was difficult then to imagine that only 24 hours later the Australians would themselves be out in the field getting toasted by the remorseless Queensland sun.

Chappell scored most of the 17 runs which came off the first two overs after lunch from Croft and Roberts. Soon afterwards he stroked Garner to mid-wicket to reach 50 off 108 balls with six boundaries. A straight drive and a superb square-cut, with the bat coming down on the ball like a wood-chopper's axe, brought him two more fours and raised the 100 partnership in 118 minutes, 58 of them to Chappell. A drive through extra-cover gave Laird his fifth boundary and his first Test 50 and there seemed little reason for their progress to be interrupted. But the West Indian fast bowlers, determined to disprove the widely-aired views in Australian papers that they were a dispirited team about to 'burst apart at the seams', never gave up, generally banging the ball in a little short of a length but not overdoing the bouncer. Eventually Roberts, with the first ball of a new spell, took the vital wicket of the Australian captain, who hooked hard but straight to King at square-leg.

When Croft, who greatly deserved another wicket to show for his sustained speed and hostility, followed up by bowling Hughes as he played a defensive stroke which lacked conviction, the West Indies were able to go into tea in much better heart, with Australia faltering a little at 180 for four. As it happened, they were never again to take control.

Only one more wicket fell before the end of the first day and in two respects it was unfortunate for Australia. Laird had played so soundly and bravely for just over five hours that he thoroughly deserved a century in his first Test innings. But he was given out caught behind off a lifting delivery from Garner. Umpire Crafter's decision was entirely understandable because Laird plays with the bat very close to his pad and there was a slight but definite deviation of the ball on its path to the wicket-keeper. The television replay *from behind* seemed to show that Laird's bat had come fractionally inside the line of the ball which had instead deviated off his thigh. He had not given a chance in an admirable innings.

No such pluck or sound technique was displayed by the long Australian tail on the second day. It was very hot (34 degrees Centigrade) from an early hour, and also intensely humid. Marsh and Hookes, the left-handed pair not out when bad light and nearby thunder and lightning had stopped play an hour early the night before, needed only to entrench themselves for an hour to keep the West Indies sweating in the heat. But Hookes, who had hitherto played with skill and circumspection, tried to hook a ball well outside his off-stump and merely succeeded in skying the ball to mid-wicket. After that it was sudden death. Marsh was given a life by Greenidge off Garner before glancing a fine catch down the legside where Murray dived to take a dream of a wicket-keeper's catch in his right glove. Lillee came in with an aluminium bat which he was marketing, but did not do his sales any good by missing a straight full-toss. Bright stuck at the crease for a little more than an hour but made only 13 before Holding yorked him. At the other end Croft was warned by umpire Crafter for bowling three successive short deliveries to Hogg, the first indication that fears of a 'bouncer war' might be justified. So far the deterrent theory – 'don't bowl bouncers at us or we'll bowl them back at you' – appeared to hold more water.

Hogg also fell to a full-toss and an hour and a half into the second day the West Indies fast bowlers had completed their job. The pitch had given them little help, and they could congratulate themselves on taking the last eight wickets for 112 runs and the last five for 39 runs on the second morning. Now it was up to the batsmen and they responded magnificently, although the subsequent story might have been different if in the nasty period of 25 minutes batting before lunch Greenidge had been caught for three from a top-edged hook off Lillee. The unfortunate spiller of a straightforward-looking chance, which may have swirled a little in the breeze, was Lillee's own partner Jeff Thomson.

Thus reprieved, Greenidge, who had a bad tour to Australia in 1975-76, began to reel off some of the formidable array of strokes which make him such a joy to watch in English county cricket. He confined himself largely to cuts and drives. Haynes, compact and muscular in a pair of cream-coloured flannels, lost nothing at all by comparison, hitting some magnificent square-cuts and cover-drives. The outfield, baked by the intense sun, was fast as an ice-rink and in a mere ten overs the West Indies had 50 on the board at a run a minute. When Chappell was forced to bring himself on for the 12th over of the innings Australia were desperate for a wicket. It came at 68 to the first ball of Lillee's second spell, delivered this time from the Vulture Street end. Greenidge played a

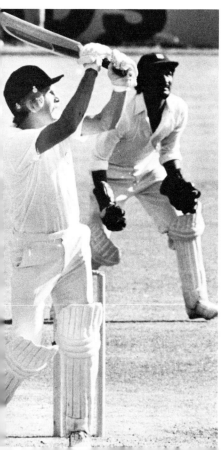

The three outstanding Australian batsmen of the season. *Above left* Greg Chappell on his way to his match-saving 100 in the first Test against the West Indies at Brisbane. *Above right* Kim Hughes: after leading Australia in India Hughes was demoted to vice-captain, but his personality helped to heal the wounds between the 'Packer men' and the 'establishment men' in the Australian team. Here he hits Botham for four in his 99 at Perth. *Left* Bruce Laird, the Australian 'discovery' of the 1979-80 season, though he was far from being a novice. Sound technique, concentration and courage earned him an average of 56 against the West Indies fast bowlers. Here he clips Holding for four during the Brisbane Test.

Above left 'Aggro' on the field – generally condemned in 1979-80 but also generally ignored by uncertain umpires and weak administrators. This was Joel Garner's hostile reaction after David Hookes had been given not out following a caught-behind appeal at Brisbane. *Above right* Colin Croft, seen during his round-the-wicket spell against Australia at Adelaide, was a prime offender in New Zealand. *Below* Alvin Kallicharran, who batted and fielded beautifully throughout the season, drives Mallett during his sparkling 106 at Adelaide.

Rodney Hogg came down to earth with a thud in 1979-80. After his sensational Test series against England the previous year he had a bad tour of India and took only two wickets in two Tests at home. This unusual appeal earned him one of them – Haynes l.b.w. in Brisbane.

Above Another wicket for the irrepressible Botham: Toohey caught behind by Taylor at Perth. Border is the non-striker. *Below* Lillee strikes back at Adelaide, having Randall brilliantly caught by Hughes. Marsh, Chappell, Border and Wiener acclaim the catch.

tentative stroke to a ball which left him and Marsh captured the first of his five victims in the innings. Haynes at once restored West Indian superiority, greeting Thomson, who had come on downwind to try to blast home the small breach which Lillee had made, with a thundering square-cut boundary. It was the duel between Lillee and Richards, however, which really compelled interest: champion versus champion, the one in the evening of his career, the other still in his prime, and from the moment that Richards played his first ball solidly to mid-off from the middle of the bat there was no question but that he would be master this time. In all the circumstances Richards played one of his finest Test innings. He was hampered from the start by the pulled muscles high on either side of his right thigh which had threatened to keep him out of the game. He knew that, with Lloyd out of the team, the responsibility on him was greater than normal and that, this being the first of only a three-match series, a major innings by him now would be of immense importance actually and psychologically. Moreover, he soon lost Haynes who, after playing the most exquisite late cover-drive, placing the ball deliberately just backward of point, was caught behind off a thin outside edge off Thomson.

Richards, however, was already in command and Kallicharran settled in quickly so the fire of the Australian fast bowlers was soon doused again. Thirteen runs came off Thomson's eighth over, eight to fiercely struck offside fours by Richards. The West Indies scored 62 from 13 overs in the first hour of their innings, 73 from only 12 in the second. Those who had come to get drunk rather than to watch the cricket began to hurl cans at one another on the Gabba hill. But there was no escaping for long from what Richards was doing to the pride of Australia's fast bowling. He limped into tea with 50 runs off 58 balls, the first landmark reached with three fours in one over from Lillee, an on-drive and two casually stroked boundaries through mid-wicket, the Viv Richards special. Between lunch and tea West Indies had scored 133 runs in 26 overs at better than five runs per over.

Australia's bowlers, weighed down by such a stroke player and by the sultry heat, now close to 100 degrees Fahrenheit, must have been glad that for the first time since the bodyline series of 1932-33 Australia had reverted to the six-ball rather than the eight-ball over. However, they did better in the last session of the day. Hogg was slow to react to a caught-and-bowled chance from Richards before he had added to his tea score, but by bowling a better line and length than 'Lillian Thomson' 'Kodogg' succeeded in keeping Richards and Kalli-charran a good deal quieter, with considerable help from Bright at the other end. Kallicharran made only 17 in the hour after tea and was then caught down the legside by Marsh off Thomson. Richards now set himself to keep his wicket intact and, despite for once missing a hook at Lillee and receiving a glancing blow on the side of the chin (he was one of the few batsmen not now wearing a helmet), he was 80 not out when the second day ended at 233 for three.

Rowe, 14 not out overnight, settled in comfortably with Richards again next morning, and Richards's muscle pains had clearly eased with a good night's rest because he was moving more freely and soon hooking anything short on either side of mid-wicket (but never behind square) with marvellous power and precision.

It was another very hot day and Australia were back on their heels again almost before they had rubbed the sleep from their eyes. Rowe hit fours off the last two balls of an over from Bright – a perfectly timed off-drive followed by the most delicate of late-cuts, whereupon Richards, not to be out-done, hit the next three balls from Hogg to the boundary too: pull, hook and cover-drive cracked from his bat in rapid succession.

A sweep for a single off Bright brought Richards his second hundred against Australia and his ninth in Tests. Hogg made some sort of riposte by bouncing a ball over Richards's intended square-cut, but two balls later the next short ball was despatched to the boundary between mid-wicket and mid-on.

Chappell himself took the responsibility of slowing things down, bowling some steady overs of medium-pace, with Lillee at half-pace resorting to the same tactics. Rowe, having played so well, became impatient and, after reaching 50 with a skilful loft over mid-wicket followed by another late-cut, hit across a ball of full length from Chappell and a stand of 119 was over. This time Australia followed up quickly. It was King's misfortune to come in just as the new ball was due and he never looked like surviving for long against Lillee, who, though his thatch of dark hair was thinning and his pace was far less than it had once been, was still capable of dangerous movement with the new ball.

Murray stuck with Richards until lunch but Richards was out for 140 early in the afternoon, an inside edge off Lillee giving Marsh the chance to take his fifth and best catch, and Australia worked their way gradually through the tail until Croft walked out at number eleven to join Garner not long before tea. In the next 81 minutes Garner flayed a tired attack while Croft, his hands gripping the bottom of the bat handle as if his life depended on it, blocked stubbornly. Garner, starting with a searing straight drive which would certainly have broken Bright's fingers if he had been unwise enough to get them in the way, used his freakish reach, considerable strength and (like all Barbadians) his knowledge of the essentials of batting to surpass his previous highest Test score. His 60 included four huge sixes, two to the legside, two almost straight, off the three left-arm slow bowlers Bright, Border and Hookes. It needed a somewhat dubious l.b.w. decision to end his fun and Australia's torment.

Australia at least ended the day honourably. McCosker and Laird, faced with more than an hour's batting, survived an aggressive opening burst by Roberts and Holding (who both, perhaps, strove to bowl too fast) and also reduced by 30 the deficit of 173 before a sudden build-up of cloud swiftly gobbled up the setting sun and ended play 25 minutes early.

For those watching as well as those playing, the enervating heat was a severe trial, and no one welcomed the agreement to play the Australia versus West Indies Tests without the traditional rest day. The last time a series of five-day Tests had been played without any break was the one between India and West Indies in 1948-49.

The West Indian fast bowlers, however, had plenty of spring in their heels on the fourth morning. Holding in particular, although he often ran in off a run much shorter than his normal 25-yard sprint to the stumps, bowled faster than anyone and in the sixth over of the day he accounted for McCosker with a fast, short delivery which a startled batsman helped onto his stumps via the inside edge of the bat. Seven overs later, when the total was 55, Border drove at what appeared to be a half-volley from Garner and sliced the ball well to the left of

Richards at third slip, only for that remarkable athlete to grasp the ball at the full extent of his left arm.

The combination of Chappell and Laird, however, again put spine into the Australian batting. Laird might twice have been out before lunch, once when he played a bouncer from Holding onto his leg-stump without dislodging a bail and then when he rocked back to avoid another bouncer and his helmet fell off but just missed the stumps. Chappell's luck came later when Holding returned fifty minutes after lunch to start the sparks flying again after a period of twenty minutes without a run. First Laird hit a four and a three through the offside, then Chappell drove at a ball of full length, edged fast but straight to Kallicharran at first slip and survived the chance. He was then 21.

Laird reached another laudable fifty twenty minutes before tea after four and a half hours. He had confirmed himself as a sound, gutsy but limited player whose scoring strokes were confined to push-drives between cover and mid-on, an occasional cut and a productive lofted legside shot off his legs. Chappell followed Laird to *his* second fifty of the match ten minutes after and Laird sent Australia to their tea in good heart by cover-driving and lofting Roberts for two fours in a tired-looking over to hoist the second century partnership of the game between these two men.

The West Indies owed their only other success of the day to the fact that Holding had joined the injured Richards in the dressing-room for temporary repairs to tired limbs. Derek Parry and Malcolm Marshall were the substitutes and it was the lissom Marshall who dived forward at backward point to hold a fine low catch as Laird cut at a ball from Garner and failed to keep the ball on the ground. He had been in just over five hours for his 75 and in his first two Test innings had blunted the West Indian fast attack for ten hours and five minutes in all, a remarkable feat of concentration.

Hughes, vice-captain in name but not in authority, one felt – the WSC players were still a group within a group who the previous evening had been meeting together to talk about contracts and who were still partners in a professional players' association which non-WSC players had not joined – seemed, like Border before him, a little uncertain. He essayed one risky hook off Croft and middled another brilliantly before settling

down into the necessary defensive vein. Australia were in the
lead again now (16 ahead at Laird's dismissal) but the need was
still to occupy the crease. A weary Chappell knew this well
and kept his head down admirably. Occasionally he leaned into
an elegant straight drive but allowed himself no liberties.
Murray took the new ball twenty minutes from the end, having
waited ten overs longer than necessary, and used Kallicharran's occasional off-spin for a time. But Holding and Roberts
bowled only three ill-directed overs in that time.

Chappell was 97 not out and Hughes 16 not out when the
final day of what had seemed a very long game began on
another sunny and sultry morning. Mercifully, the power-
strike which for two days had deprived Queenslanders of
light, cooking heat, and above all the use of fridges and
air-conditioners, was over. Even Channel Nine had been
off the air for a while: Kerry Packer might now control
Australian cricket but without electricity even he had no
power!

The West Indies, determined to win a series in Australia for
the first time and knowing that their great chance in this match
had almost slipped through their fingers, had to throw everything into their assault with the new ball. The pitch was getting
deader by the minute and there was no spinner in their
monotonous attack to use the dry white turf. But they took an
hour and twenty minutes to take the first wicket of the day and
by lunchtime the match was moribund. Not that the first
session of the day was without incident. It began with a quick
flurry of runs, Hughes hitting Croft for two offside fours and
Chappell then reaching his 15th Test hundred and his fifth
against the West Indies with a square-cut boundary off
Holding.

When he was 103 Chappell lofted an on-drive off Roberts
hard and low to Marshall, fielding substitute for Richards at
mid-on. The chance was not taken and Chappell celebrated
with two glorious cover-drives off Croft. But the latter hit back
by bowling Chappell with a beauty, an inswinger which nipped
the other way off the seam to take the off-stump. Australia
were then 124 ahead. Hookes survived an appeal for l.b.w.
first ball and then a more vehement one in the next over when
he pushed forward to Garner and Murray exultantly claimed a
catch. Garner strode up the pitch to tower over Hookes with a

meaningful glare whilst umpire Crafter (a most amiable man, incidentally, who once played League cricket in Lancashire) came humbly down the pitch having called 'over' to hand Garner back his cap. It was taken, rather than seized, by Garner but his feelings were in no way concealed.

At lunch Australia were 320 for four, 147 ahead and in the clear. The afternoon had significance only for certain individuals, and especially for Kim Hughes, who reached his second successive Test hundred at the Gabba, his third in Test cricket and his highest, surpassing the excellent 129 he had made on the same ground against England the year before. It was by far the most entertaining innings by an Australian in the game, and although he had some luck with lofted hook shots he also hit some magnificent blows including a six to mid-wicket off King. He also hit 17 fours before Chappell declared with an hour of the match left.

It was anything but a dull finish. Greenidge holed out to Thomson for a duck; Hogg bowled Rowe for 3 and two balls later had Haynes l.b.w. for 4 in an over in which he also bowled three no-balls; and then Lillee, never likely to be out of any act, bowled five no-balls in one over and was spoken to sternly by Chappell for firing off a lightning delivery while Marsh was standing up to the stumps. But all this hectic action came too late. The match ended in the first draw in a Test in Australia since the one against Pakistan in December 1976 when Australia had not risked a late chase for runs. They had done the same in similar circumstances against England at Melbourne in 1975. Between that Melbourne game and this one at Brisbane 26 Tests had passed with only one draw. The lasting nature of Jack Macandrew's pitch was one good reason, but others were the West Indies decision to leave their only specialist spinner out of the eleven and their failure to hold the chances which Greg Chappell had offered at 21 and 103 in his second innings. Australia, thanks largely to Chappell, Laird and Hughes, had earned an honourable draw: West Indies had missed a rare opportunity. It is also arguable that they might have won had their bowlers had the traditional rest day in which to recuperate.

The Australian selectors announced two changes for the international matches against England and West Indies at the weekend, recalling Doug Walters (still only 33 but a Test cricketer for 15 years) in place of Dymock and introducing Julian Wiener, the 24-year-old Victorian opening batsman in place of McCosker. Wiener, whose parents are Austrian, had scored consistently, if not prolifically, for two seasons of Shield cricket and played with a straighter bat than McCosker, who had always been an outstanding onside player but less good around his off-stump. Wiener had made a good impression against England the previous season, and had the virtue also of bowling off-spin on occasions.

The Test twelve for Perth showed only one change, McCosker giving way to Wiener. Bright was fortunate to retain his place ahead of Higgs, who had just bowled Victoria to a Shield success with 12 wickets in the match against Western Australia.

Chapter Four

GEOFF BOYCOTT'S RISE, IAN CHAPPELL'S FALL

Whilst Australia and West Indies were grappling in Brisbane, England were further preparing for the first major date in their diary, the first Test against Australia at Perth. During the Brisbane Test England defeated Tasmania by 100 runs with two balls to spare, then moved to Adelaide where the batting of Geoff Boycott and the antics of Ian Chappell dominated another sparsely attended match. Seven days' cricket played by England in Adelaide drew a total of 3,673 spectators. In Hobart the saddest thing that happened was the decision to send Mike Hendrick home because his damaged shoulder was showing no sign of improvement; the oddest occurrence was a gale-force wind of 25 knots stopping play on the second day; and the best events took place on the first and last days of the game. On the first Geoff Boycott confirmed his good form with a chanceless 101 not out after Brian Davison, the Rhodesian who plays for Leicestershire and had taken over as Tasmania's captain in the absence of Jack Simmons (in his benefit year for Lancashire), had put England in to bat. Gooch also batted well for 51. Then, on the third day, Derek Underwood, after surviving a battering from the promising Robbie Knight, who hit a brilliant 74 whilst only 13 runs came at the other end, finished with 7 for 66 and 10 for 77 in the match.

Hendrick's departure gave Graham Stevenson his big chance. This exuberant Yorkshireman was no direct substitute for Hendrick, the most accurate fast-medium seam bowler in the world, but he had enthusiasm, strength and youthful stamina to offer instead. He played his first match against South Australia in Adelaide and began quite promisingly with a wicket in each innings.

It was Boycott and Chappell, however, who made the headlines. Boycott and Brearley put on 174 on a perfect pitch in hot weather after the latter had won the toss. In Prior and

McLellan the State side had a hostile opening attack, but the vastly experienced England pair played them with comfort. At one point Brearley squeezed a ball into the ground and an appeal was made for a catch. Brearley hastily told the fielder he had hit the ball into the ground; at the end of the over Chappell said laconically from the side of his mouth: 'We can do without the ball-by-ball commentary, Mike.'

Chappell made another kind of comment after lunch when, in order to draw attention to England's continued refusal to accept Australian proposals for a limit of five fielders on the leg-side, he himself bowled the first over with nine fielders on the leg-side. It was a harmless enough gesture, but in the circumstances it was hardly wise – Chappell was playing his first game since his three-week suspension for swearing at an umpire. If he was to get back into the Test side – and it was widely felt that Australia still needed his batting skill even if he had virtually ruled himself out as captain – he needed most of all to get his head down and play a big innings against England. Instead it was Boycott who took the opportunity to confirm his good form, making a chanceless 110 in 229 minutes with 16 well-timed boundaries. This, his 117th first-class hundred, brought him level with Sir Donald Bradman's career total and Boycott was playing with such composure that his disappointing tour the previous year seemed like a distant bad dream.

Boycott's poor form then had been caused partly by technical problems, especially concerning the movement of his feet, and partly by his worries following his loss of the Yorkshire captaincy and the death of his mother. Now it was Chappell who had domestic problems and they perhaps explained his irrational behaviour on the second day of the match when his turn came to bat. Facing Ian Botham for the second ball of his innings, Chappell lost sight of a short-pitched ball in some television scaffolding behind the bowler's arm and ran for a leg-bye when the ball glanced off his body. When he got to the other end the umpire, Graham McLeod, standing in his first first-class match, called dead ball on the grounds that Chappell had not been playing a stroke or taking evasive action and could not therefore run for a leg-bye.

Chappell later called this 'an incompetent decision by an incompetent umpire'. Most of the other players agreed that he had indeed taken evasive action and that the leg-bye should have stood. But what a trivial matter upon which to place in jeopardy a distinguished cricket career! Chappell first argued the issue with McLeod, then angrily threw his bat to the ground. Botham pitched short again next ball and Chappell swung wildly to be caught behind off the glove. Later, in the field, Chappell threw the sweater and cap of his opening bowler Ross McLellan at the umpire and declined to pick them up when McLeod said the game would not start until he did. McLeod's senior partner, Max O'Connell, intervened to suggest to his colleague that they should start the game and forget the trivial argument. Trivial it all undoubtedly was, but this was no behaviour for a captain of a State side – let alone a Test team – and when McLeod reported Chappell to the South Australian Cricket Association the secretary, Neil Blundell, asked Sir Donald Bradman (Adelaide's most famous citizen) to inquire into the matter. His findings were passed on to the ACB who this time gave Chappell a suspended sentence of six weeks, one which would only come into force if he misbehaved again. Perhaps this was a sign of clemency and indicative of official sympathy for a fallen idol who had run into hard times; or perhaps it was a pragmatic decision which effectively meant: 'Don't rock the boat again, Ian, because we may yet need you to play again for your country.' Sure enough, he was recalled to the Australian side within a fortnight.

The Adelaide match finished in a draw despite two declarations by Brearley and one by Chappell. The key to any cricket match is the pitch, and most of the strips encountered by England on the tour so far were quite different from the grassy ones which had so delighted the likes of Hendrick and Hogg the year before. In fact England managed to get close to losing to South Australia for the second season running after Brearley had shuffled his batting cards in the second innings to give everyone some practice. England were rescued from the perilous position of 76 for six in their second innings – a mere 102 runs on – by Miller and Boycott.

Miller, who relishes a crisis, made 71 but during the course of his innings strained his back as he twisted to evade a hard drive back along the pitch by Boycott. This was to have consequences which the latter had not intended, for, having made a superb 63 not out and hit the spinners with many a confident blow through mid-wicket or extra-cover, Boycott had to accept the selectors' decision to leave him out of the eleven for the first one-day international staged at Melbourne. Accordingly, at eight o'clock on the morning of Saturday, 8 December, the most dedicated cricketer in history was practising in the nets to the bowling of his young Yorkshire colleague Graham Stevenson. When the players arrived an hour later, however, they told Boycott that he would be playing after all because Miller's back was no better.

The game was due to start at ten o'clock and already the first few of a crowd of 24,726 were taking up their positions in the great stadium. Many came fully expecting to see the Poms put in their place in this first meeting between the two sides since England had defeated Australia in the first match of the Prudential World Cup in June. Some would also have been aware that they were to see Boycott playing the Lillee/Thomson combination for the first time. But if they came to bury the old man they stayed to praise him.

Brearley won the toss, put Australia in and got just the start he wanted. By the eighth over the new pair of Laird and Wiener had come and gone, but Greg Chappell, walking in at 15 for two, played a beautiful innings of 92, defying all the swiftly alternated variations of England's attack and the defensive field-settings with a masterly display of his own. In particular he launched a successful attack on Underwood, often his tormentor in the past. Despite all that Brearley did to contain him, and the immensity of the Melbourne outfield, Chappell hit ten boundaries and consistently probed the gaps for ones and twos. Border supported him well but fell to a wild stroke and a brilliant running catch by Willey, and Hughes was scoring just as fast as his captain when he was 'accidentally' stumped down the leg-side by Bairstow, the ball bouncing off the wicket-keeper's body with the batsman stranded. Australia finished with 207 for 9, a total which on a pitch as bland and slow as this one promised an even contest.

So it proved, although England ought to have won more easily than they eventually did after Boycott and Randall had given them an ideal start. Boycott said later that he was unusually nervous, not having been in the side originally, but he did not seem so when Lillee and Hogg launched their attack amidst a crescendo of roaring voices. The first few overs were calmly played by both men, and then Boycott, much to the amazement of those who had witnessed his strokeless struggles of the previous tour, sailed into a confident square-cut off Thomson and followed it with a searing cover-drive.

Randall had made only 28 of an opening stand of 71 when he was l.b.w to Bright, and in the next three-quarters of an hour Boycott and Willey took command, pushing up the run-rate to the required 4.2 per over. Hogg returned and Boycott's confidence was underlined by his willingness to hook him. In fact, however, this proved his undoing because having twice played dangerous hooks his third attempt came off the top edge to Lillee at deep fine-leg. Boycott had scored 68 off only 85 balls with seven fours, and Australians, quick to criticise him in the past, were equally quick to praise him now.

England's score was 134 when Boycott was out but the crowd had certainly not given up hope and, urged on by deafening cries from the 'outer', Hogg followed up by having Willey caught down the leg-side by an acrobatic Marsh – possibly an unlucky decision against the batsman – and then Botham caught at mid-off when the latter again applied too little thought to what he was doing. Since Gooch had been needlessly run out when looking in the opposite direction as Gower called him for a sharp but legitimate run, England were suddenly in danger of collapse.

When Brearley walked out at number seven the score was 148 for five in the 39th over. Gower played and missed three or four times in an agonisingly uncertain start to his innings, then effortlessly lifted a ball from Chappell over the long-on boundary. Brearley, like Boycott before him, played better than anyone expected him to. The target was reduced to 25 in the last six overs. Then Gower was caught off a top-edged hook and the tension began afresh. 21 runs were needed off five overs. Brearley continued to play with admirable coolness, timing his attacking strokes well, and Bairstow for the first time fully justified his inclusion ahead of Taylor. When Brearley was out in the penultimate over only three more runs were needed. A drive from Bairstow off Lillee's last ball settled it and the little Yorkshire tank sprinted off with both arms held aloft in jubilation. England had won by three wickets with six balls to spare and the underdogs were – for the time being – top-dogs.

The following day an even bigger crowd, 39,183, saw perhaps the best individual innings of the whole Australian season. Viv Richards had been called to Melbourne from Sydney, where he was having daily treatment on his torn hip muscles. In the words of their manager Willie Rodriguez the West Indies 'had to win this game'. This must have put increased pressure on Richards but he appeared quite untroubled by it when his innings began in the ninth over after Chappell had asked West Indies to bat. This was about the last decision which the Australian captain made voluntarily because once Richards had cover-driven two boundaries and swung a third to leg in Thomson's first over 'Smokin' Joe' was in total control. Driving, cutting and pulling with awesome power he hit 153 off 131 balls, striking 16 boundaries and a vast six off Border. Richards and Haynes put on 205 in 34 overs against eight different Australian bowlers and the yellow-capped fielders hurtled in every direction over the immense outfield like a ragged column of soldiers lost in the desert.

Greg Chappell briefly gave Australian supporters hope when he scored 31 skilful runs off 21 balls but the mathematical odds – Australia needed to keep up a rate of 5.66 an over to win – were always against his team and long before they had finished their 48 overs (only 48 had been bowled in the morning session so the total was reduced by two) still 80 runs adrift, attention had switched to the numerous fights breaking out at the Southern End. In the two days' cricket at the MCG police arrested 75 people for drunk and disorderly behaviour, obscene exposure or abusive language. A streaker invaded the field on both days and the second one felt the blade of Chappell's angry willow on his backside.

The glorification of the pop element in WSC cricket had undoubtedly encouraged the crowd's loutishness. This perhaps paled in comparison with the deeds of football mobs in England but it was nonetheless deplorable at cricket matches. When England and Australia met again at Sydney two days after the West Indies victory over Australia, no one was allowed to bring alcohol into the ground. This did not deter the Sydney public from coming in large numbers again, and the crowd at its peak was 15,083. Inside the ground the hillsiders were able to buy cartons of a dozen cans, so perhaps the only difference was that the SCG Trust and their caterers made greater profits. On the face of it behaviour was improved, and the police managed to keep intruders off the pitch, but more than one can was thrown in anger. Bob Taylor was hit by a metal staple and Ian Botham by a half-full can on the back of the neck.

Australia made four changes in their team, Rick Darling replacing Bruce Laird in order largely to sharpen up the fielding, Max Walker returning in place of Ray Bright, Trevor Laughlin taking over from Rodney Hogg, who had a slight back strain, and Doug Walters again replacing David Hookes.

Although Walker fully justified his return with a steady spell of ten overs off the reel after Brearley had won the toss, Australia were soon running in all directions as another bland Sydney pitch drew what sting remained of their once ferocious fast bowlers. This game was an even bigger personal triumph for the revitalised Boycott. He had one great piece of luck when he was 16, Darling at extra-cover muffing a straightforward catch off Walker, but thereafter he played with a confidence and command that was marvellous to behold. His innings of 105 contained one other much harder chance when he was 76 but also a handsome array of off-drives and every legside stroke, except the hook, from the glance to the on-drive, more than once played with complete certainty over the top of the field. Chappell seemed again to be bereft of ideas, and no bowler came along with an inspired spell to rescue him.

Boycott was once more given splendid support by Peter Willey, the silent Geordie who was making such a success of his belated first tour. During the course of another inventive innings full of aggressive and well-timed strokes Willey pulled a muscle in his left calf, but he knew that he was needed as a bowler and cheerfully went onto the field to play his part. After Willey had made 64 off 58 balls, England's middle order came and went quickly in the chase for quick runs; one enormous hit for six by Bairstow off Lillee took the rate for the innings to 5.4 per over, and this was to prove far too great a task for Australia.

Darling and Wiener, yet another new opening pair for a country badly needing a settled partnership, gave Australia a sensible start, but Darling was soon pressing for runs a little too anxiously against tight bowling and fielding and as soon as he was out Australia collapsed, losing five wickets for six runs.

Willis, bowling his most hostile spell on the tour so far, took two; Willey captured two more thanks in Wiener's case to a superb legside stumping, and Chappell was run out by Gower. Laughlin, with an excellent innings of 74, and Walters, who sparkled during his innings of 34 to the delight of the Sydney crowd, saved some face for their team but England won by the crushing margin of 72 runs. The contest had long been settled when Randall, that marvellous natural clown, brought the house down by trying on a succession of different hats lent by spectators, finishing with a policeman's peaked cap under which he sauntered about in hilarious fashion with his elastic body contorting into all sorts of silly walks. John Cleese himself could not have done it better. Randall finished off the evening by bowling the 48th over and Laughlin obligingly holed out.

So it was that Australia's cricketers travelled from east to west licking their wounds, while England's men made the same long journey to Perth in a state of high good humour. England's momentum was going to take some stopping, but Australia knew that Perth, the fastest pitch in Australia, would give Lillee and Thomson a great opportunity. Hogg was unable to join them in the final eleven because of his inflamed vertebrae, so Dymock at last got his chance.

England preferred Willey to Gooch at number three in the order and fielded a balanced attack with Willis, Dilley and Botham to bowl fast and Underwood, Miller and Willey to spin the ball. With Brearley at number seven the batting order also looked reassuringly long. But with Willey at three and Miller at five, it was a case of quantity not quality.

Chapter Five

LILLEE – CHILD AND CHAMPION

A gentle ripple blew across England's calm waters on the eve of the first Test. Geoff Boycott, who seemed to be in such a buoyant and relaxed mood, was unfortunately overheard by a local reporter when making an unexpectedly testy comment to his captain during practice. Boycott, who was apparently still resentful at being replaced as vice-captain by Willis and overlooked as a tour selector, was asked by Brearley for the benefit of his experience of the Perth pitch. Boycott was quoted as replying in the bluntest terms that as he had given his advice in the past and it had been ignored he had no intention of offering any now. Once the hasty rejoinder had found its way into the local evening paper it was public news and Boycott's name was once again on the back page of every popular newspaper in London the following morning.

It was an incident which quickly passed when the fascinating opening day's cricket began. Brearley won the toss and, after taking the advice of other senior players more willing to proffer an opinion, he asked Australia to bat first on a bright, breezy day.

The pitch, the last Test strip prepared by the retiring WACA curator Ron Abbott (who was to be succeeded by John Maley, the inventor of the 'concrete transplant' pitch used by WSC at VFL Park in Melbourne), was soon confirmed as fast, bouncy and at times uncomfortable to bat on. Veins of green grass gave some movement off the seam all day, and with the prevailing Perth south-westerly blowing in from the Swan River all day there was some swing as well, especially for Ian Botham, who began with an admirable fourteen-over spell from the Grandstand end. He had a brief rest just before lunch but then came straight on again afterwards to bowl for another hour.

Little went right for Australia in the first hour. Laird was l.b.w. in Botham's second over, trapped on the back foot by a ball which leapt back from the off. Border, after playing and missing frequently outside the off-stump, survived a most convincing appeal for a catch behind the wicket, only to succumb to an l.b.w. decision by the same umpire, Max O'Connell, two balls later. Then, at 20, Greg Chappell – having been discomforted by a sharply rising delivery from Willis the previous ball – called Wiener for a legside single only for the young opener to lose his wicket in his first Test in the most unfortunate manner: run out. Dilley, picking up quickly at mid-wicket and hitting the stumps with his throw, was the man responsible. By a strange coincidence Dilley's parents had put Wiener up for several months in 1977 when the young Victorian of Austrian descent had spent the summer in England playing for Kent Second Eleven. Dilley himself, at 20 years 7 months, younger by 94 days than Brian Statham when he made his début for England and the youngest to do so since Brian Close in 1949, was finding it difficult to believe that he had become a fully-fledged England cricketer. 'I have only just woken up to the fact that I really am on a full England tour,' he said, 'let alone playing in a Test.'

Dilley betrayed some nerves in his first spell downwind, having been given the new ball ahead of Bob Willis, who kept a careful eye on him for most of the day from mid-on or mid-off. But Dilley looked as though he could handle everything himself. He had come a long way since the day when, as a 13-year-old schoolboy, he had approached Alan Knott as the England wicket-keeper left the cricket ground at Dartford and asked him how he could become a professional cricketer. Knott referred him to Colin Page, the Kent manager, sitting next to him in his car when Dilley approached. Dilley was told to come to the holiday nets. He began playing for Kent under-16s as a medium-pace change bowler, climbed to the under-19s after taking six for 19 against a Dutch touring team, and in 1977 represented Kent for the first time. Now, after a mere five weeks in Australia, he had taken the last step from a promising fast-medium bowler to one of genuine pace, worthy of opening the bowling in a Test. Moreover he was lucky enough to start on the fastest Test pitch in the world, though he had to wait until mid-afternoon to claim his first Test wicket. Australia were rescued by a marvellously positive innings from Kim

Hughes. His resuscitation of the innings began in company with a subdued Greg Chappell, who was in one of those pale and listless moods he sometimes has when he looks as though he might melt away into nothing, like a nervous ghost surprised in the attic.

It was Hughes who hit the first assertive strokes of the day, striking Botham for successive fours with a straight drive followed by a square-cut. There is a handsome full-bloodedness about Hughes's attacking strokes, a gymnastic flamboyance which is almost West Indian. Even his forward defensive shot is pleasing to watch, a model of neatness and rectitude with the head over the ball, the body inclined forward and the bat angled down. He had made 37 by lunch. Chappell – once shaking off his chains to hook Willis to square-leg – was 16 not out, and as a bagpipe band, appropriate for Perth and a good deal more peaceful than the rock-and-roll blasted out at maximum volume in the intervals of the one-day internationals, entertained the modest crowd of 9,493 at lunch, the Australians could hope for a more prosperous afternoon.

At 88, however, Ian Botham, the young lion, broke the partnership between Australia's captain and vice-captain as Chappell pushed towards point and Boycott at third slip gobbled a straightforward catch as if he had been a specialist slip all his life. The pitch was still giving generous bounce and just enough movement and Brearley must have wished at times that England had found a place for Lever, who had bowled so well at Perth on the last tour. Lever's form had been disappointing but he would surely have revelled in these conditions.

Toohey, restored to the side in place of the injured Hookes, settled in patiently but, as they had a year before, England's bowlers harried his off-stump ruthlessly and he never really looked at ease. He miscued a hook at Willis, only for the bowler to miss a relatively easy catch off his own bowling, and held on for another half-hour as Hughes, needing some luck outside the off-stump, cut, drove and hooked his way past 50. Once Botham had bowled himself out Brearley used Willis and Dilley downwind and Miller and Underwood into the breeze. It was Dilley who eventually had Toohey, a hasty hook sending a curling catch to Underwood, who made no mistake at deep fine-leg.

·Marsh and Hughes now contributed the second substantial stand of the innings, either side of tea. Marsh began with a heavily clubbed six over mid-wicket off Miller and a crisp off-drive against Dilley, but he also took some ungainly heaves at Miller, trusting that he would not be given out when the ball struck his front pad, as it frequently did.

Hughes was eleven runs from a second successive Test century at tea, and only one tantalising run short when he pulled Underwood hard to Brearley at square-leg. He had batted a little under four hours, hit ten fours and saved his team from a total failure. He more than deserved that extra run.

England would probably have finished the innings on the first day had not Marsh survived a stumping chance off Underwood which Taylor would normally have accepted in his sleep. Taylor was a little short of match practice and perhaps nervous with Bairstow pushing him hard for his Test place. At any rate Marsh, missed at 27, stayed a good deal longer and reached 42 before Brearley took the new ball as soon as it was due and Taylor made amends with a fine leg-side catch off Dilley. Bright, having done a very useful job, promptly gave Botham a fourth and well-deserved wicket, and Australia ended the day at 232 for 8.

The second day began with an extraordinary incident, involving one of the biggest prima donnas that cricket has known. Against the wishes of his captain Lillee went out to bat with the aluminium bat which he was marketing. He had taken the precaution of getting written confirmation from the Australian Board that the bat was legal. When he first played the ball with a metallic clang it was quite amusing. But not for long. Chappell sent out Hogg with two alternative wooden bats which Lillee refused to accept. At the same time Brearley objected to the bat as well on the grounds that it was causing damage to the ball – 'It looked as though it had twice been hit against a concrete wall' – and the umpires told Lillee to change it because it amounted in their view to unfair play under Law 46. Lillee strode into the pavilion and emerged several minutes later with the same aluminium bat. I understand from a dressing-room witness that he was urged not to change the bat by Rodney Marsh. When asked why he had not left the aluminium bat behind the team manager John Edwards said:

'That is the great unanswered question. We thought he *had* changed it.' Lillee brushed past the umpires as he returned to the middle with a defiant strut. The umpires again told Lillee to change the bat and eventually Chappell came out with a wooden replacement and, without fuss, told him to use it. Lillee threw the offending article twenty yards towards the pavilion in a final petulant gesture of defiance, designed, it seemed, to make sure that he would be on every front and back page in every Sunday paper. It was marvellous free advertising as far as Lillee was concerned and Tony Greig promptly predicted that the bat would outsell all others within a year. But the immediate point at issue was that Lillee was disobeying both his captain and the umpire's orders. The crowd's reaction was hostile, even though Lillee was a local hero. One spectator summed it up well: 'Who's running this game, Lillee,' he yelled, 'you or the umpires?'

Lillee himself later seemed totally unaware of the deeper issues involved. He put out a statement denying that his tantrums over the bat were part of an advertising stunt, although in an ABC interview he said he had used the bat to 'expose it for the Christmas sales'. He also said that the bat did not damage the ball and that its use was perfectly legal. The first matter was clearly one for debate, and further tests needed to be carried out, although not in a Test match. The second point, that the bat was strictly legal, was true, although from April 1980 any non-wood bats were to be outlawed under the new code of laws. Yet there was no doubt that the idea of a cheaper and virtually indestructible cricket bat was a good one.

Lillee's crimes were (a) to disobey his captain, (b) to argue at length with the umpires and (c) to use a Test match as a market-place. He gave an appalling example to those young players who admired his cricket and looked to him for an example. He deserved, but did not receive, immediate official censure and severe punishment. Eventually, however, as will be related in the next chapter, the Australian Board reacted to the unanimous Anglo-Australian condemnation of his behaviour.

Lillee played well enough for a time when he finally agreed to continue but Botham removed both the overnight batsmen (Dymock being the other one) to finish with well-deserved figures of 6 for 78. In his 22 Test matches he had now taken five or more wickets in a Test innings eleven times. But he was soon to be upstaged.

England's limited-over successes had all been based upon sound opening partnerships, but when Boycott and Randall opened the innings together in the Test match the result was disastrous, both of them departing for ducks as Dennis Lillee enjoyed a final fling on the ground where he first announced himself as one of the great fast bowlers by taking 8 for 29 against Gary Sobers's World XI in the 1971-72 season.

Racing in downwind from the Swan River end, his dark, hawkish features set for the kill, Lillee soon had the crowd back on his side. Randall, instead of shuffling across his stumps as normal, backed away uncertainly as the first ball, a no-ball, whistled towards him. He seemed to be expecting a bouncer or to be playing to some preordained plan not to play at anything short, which on this bouncy pitch would be certain to fly over the stumps. To the third ball, pitched to a good length on his off-stump, he again moved back towards the leg-stump, took a late stab at the ball and edged it to second slip where Kim Hughes held a marvellous low catch in his right hand. Jubilation for Australia, consternation for England.

Willey showed no sign of nerves in his first overseas Test, but England were asking much of a batsman not accustomed to a place higher than number five in the Northamptonshire batting order. He stood up to Lillee well, though a shout for l.b.w. and another optimistic one for a catch behind added to the atmosphere of crisis. Boycott, meanwhile, dealt capably enough with Dymock's first two overs. But when Willey, with nine to his name, got to the other end he edged to first slip a ball angled across his body.

Now it was Boycott's turn. He had been in for half an hour without scoring, but also without playing a single false stroke, when Lillee blasted a ball through his defensive back-stroke. The appeal was Perth-shattering and umpire Weser, with whom Boycott had had a contretemps the year before, flung his index finger towards the sky without a second's hesitation. England were 14 for three.

Gower, nonchalantly caressing the ball through the cover gap, restored some heart to his team for a while, and Miller, coming in at number five (like Willey, higher than his normal county position), held on until lunch, not without the

occasional agonising spar outside his off-stump against Lillee.
It was with the fifth ball of the last over before lunch that
Lillee took his third wicket as Gower went back and edged to
the wicket-keeper.

Brearley had been intending to bat at number seven but it
was he who walked out with Miller when play began again on a
sunny, breezy afternoon. England were 41 for four. Lillee
continued after lunch with the wind behind, whilst Dymock
battled into the wind from the Grandstand end at which
Botham had bowled so well. Perhaps belatedly Thomson came
on after Lillee's ten overs had earned him three for 35.
Brearley had emerged from a bad patch in which he three
times played and missed at Lillee, to bat with admirable
composure and judgement. As usual both he and Miller,
having played himself in, should have perished to a limp push
outside his off-stump in Thomson's third over, Hughes cling-
ing on to a fine catch to his left at second slip.

Botham wasted no time in showing his class, driving and
hooking the tireless Dymock, but at 90 England reached their
nadir when Botham drove on the up at Thomson and hit
straight into Toohey's safe hands at extra-cover. Brearley and
Taylor now used all their experience and patience to work
England inch by inch towards the light which was then barely
visible from the depths of the hole into which they had
tumbled. Taylor had been in the middle for just under an hour
when he padded up to Chappell and lost his off-stump as the
ball carried in off the seam. It was the last bad moment of the
day for England. From 123 for seven at tea, Brearley guided
his side to 177 at stumps, finding a partner full of character and
resolve in the young man of Kent, Graham Dilley. Obeying his
orders and taking heart from Brearley's rock-like resistance at
the other end, Dilley used a straight bat to repulse all that
Lillee, Thomson, Dymock, Chappell and finally Bright could
send down. Runs came only very slowly, but occupation of the
crease was the main object and as the ball grew softer and the
bowlers more tired it became clear that England had pulled
back into the match. Half an hour before the end Brearley hit
Lillee hard at Laird's knee where he stood at short-leg, a
chance in name only. Shortly afterwards he drove Dymock
square for four to reach 50 after 228 minutes. At the close he
was 56 not out, Dilley 21 not out, and England were 67 behind.

The final hour of the day was marred by more fighting in the crowd, some of it taking place in the outfield. Lillee appeared personally to incite some hostile reaction when he barged into two foolish youths running around the boundary with a Union Jack. One was grasped by a policeman, the other by two members of the crowd who sprang upon him and wrestled him to the ground.

The third day began with the unexpected statement that the umpires, having spoken to Dennis Lillee and the Australian manager John Edwards, would be making no special report about Lillee's behaviour the previous day. The statement said that the matter had been resolved, but the umpires still had to mention the matter in their match report, which left open the possibility of some action against the player by the Board.

Temporarily reprieved at least, Lillee soon took his first wicket of the morning and his 100th against England. Although no longer quite the irresistible force he had once been his performance in this innings proved that he was still a great bowler and those hundred wickets, taken entirely on covered wickets, proclaimed him as perhaps the greatest fast bowler of his time. Only Ray Lindwall had also taken 100 wickets for Australia against England since the Second World War.

Brearley was the 100th victim, caught behind by Marsh off the outside edge, like so many before him. In one of his most valuable Test innings Brearley had made 64 in 251 minutes. His end, however, was by no means the end of England's first innings because Dilley, missed when he was 25 by Marsh off Lillee, carried his bat to the end of the innings, whilst Underwood and Willis both contributed useful runs to reduce the final deficit to 16. Dymock deservedly took both the last two wickets.

So much depends, in Test cricket, upon the success of the opening batsmen. Australia had constantly shifted their opening pairs in recent seasons and now in Laird and Wiener they were testing a combination which seemed to promise well for the future. They safely negotiated seven overs before lunch and on a hot afternoon with the pitch now a little more docile they built up a strong position for their team, although had England held the half-chances the stand would have been broken long before it was. Willis was especially unlucky. He could not persuade umpire Weser to uphold what he clearly believed to be a very plumb l.b.w. decision against Wiener when the latter was 20 (he had survived an almost equally confident shout by Botham when he was 14) and he had Laird dropped in the gully by Willey when he had scored only eight. Only two balls later Laird edged Botham at catching height between Taylor and Brearley and, not long after, Laird swept a ball from Miller which struck Willey, fielding very close at forward short-leg, behind the ear. Willey was stunned, helped off the field and taken to hospital where two stitches were applied to the wound. It was that sort of afternoon for England.

Wiener in particular, however, played a fine innings. Fair-haired and strong about the shoulders, he looked both solid and straight and off the back foot he was quick to get into position to hook or to square-cut. He also showed the kind of aggression against the England spinners which the young Australian batsmen the previous year had not done. To the very first ball that Miller bowled Wiener danced three steps down the pitch and drove over the bowler's head for four, and when he had reached his first Test fifty he did the same to Underwood, this time lifting the ball for six with impressive conviction and power. In the same over, however, Underwood had his revenge, Wiener pushing a ball off his leg-stump into Randall's hands at short-leg.

Australia, comfortably placed at 99 for one at tea, lost Laird at 100 in the second over afterwards as he pushed out to Underwood and the ball turned (much to everyone's surprise) just enough to catch the edge of the bat and give Taylor a catch.

England had a chance now, with Border and Chappell both new at the crease, and Border looked much less convincing against the fast bowlers than he did against the spinners with whom, after a long tour of India, he was on very familiar terms. But, as the bowlers of both sides found throughout the match, the ball in this game had an annoying habit of missing the outside edge rather than snicking it and Border gradually became settled whilst Chappell, subdued at first, began coolly to pick up runs, stroking the ball wide of mid-on off either foot and occasionally getting right on top of the ball with his exemplary square-cut, a stroke which was once his weakest but which now looked quite fool-proof.

Border was dropped in the gully, a very fast-travelling chance to Miller off Dilley when he was 30, and England's bowlers had no further success on what had been a frustrating day for them. Botham again did most work for England, but perhaps his captain overbowled him on this occasion and underused young Dilley, who bowled only nine overs to Botham's 22. Dilley was, admittedly, very tired after his innings. Australia ended the day strongly placed at 168 for two, 184 runs ahead with two days left.

It was pleasant to have a rest day. For most of the players it was too hot to do anything except sit and relax, but for intrepid journalists it was a rare chance on a desperately busy tour to have a game of golf. The former England fast bowler Peter Loader, now one of Perth's most contented citizens, kindly organised use of the superb course at Lake Karrinup. One has putted out on Australian greens before to the accompaniment of lavatorial cackles from the kookaburras, but never before have I been watched by a kangaroo as I hovered over a tense ten-footer. The course is an oasis of green on the edge of the arid West Australian bush and it was a privilege to play there, though such was the heat – touching 100 degrees – that I was not sorry that BBC duties called me back to the city after only nine holes had been played.

The cricket at the WACA on the fourth day more than lived up to Test match tradition. There was incident a-plenty, some excellent batting and bowling, and more than one unexpected shift of fortune. At first everything went England's way. They took a wicket in the first over – Chappell's wicket – and four others before lunch. But the game so often defies logic: not another man was dismissed before tea and Australia pulled themselves away from danger.

Allan Border was the hero, batting with altogether more assurance and looking settled throughout the period during which the innings was subsiding at the other end. His hooking, pulling and driving were exemplary and he awaited the right ball to hit with nice judgement.

Chappell was dismissed in the first over of the morning, moving out to drive Underwood, finding himself stranded as the ball spun away and bounced over his attempted cut, and being smartly stumped by Taylor. Hughes survived an appeal for a catch behind off an inside edge onto his pad only three balls before he pushed out at a Botham away-cutter and edged to second slip where Miller clasped the ball to his middle a little unconvincingly. Toohey, who already knew the selectors had discarded him in favour of Ian Chappell, once again found England's tight bowling and Brearley's attacking fields too much for him. Botham persuaded him to try to relieve the pressure by hooking and a top edge to the wicket-keeper was the result.

Australia had lost three wickets in the first hour for 32 runs but Border was equal to the challenge. He drove Underwood perfectly through extra-cover for his fifth four to reach 50 and this seemed to persuade Brearley to take the new ball after 87 overs. Botham carried on cheerfully from the Grandstand end, moving the ball a little both off the seam and in the air in the muggy atmosphere, and with his first delivery with the new ball he removed Marsh as he turned a ball of good length off his toes straight to square-leg where Gower took a neat low catch.

If England were to win they needed now to finish things off quickly with the new ball but Bright did a good job in holding up Botham, a rather tired-looking Dilley, and Willis, who soon took over at the Swan River end from his young pretender. Bright was l.b.w. to Botham just before lunch when a ball kept ominously low. But this far from signified a swift end to the innings because Lillee, getting his head down with great determination and confronted after lunch by Underwood rather than an all-pace attack despite the fact that the second new ball was only twelve overs old, stayed all afternoon with Border.

Border reached a most valuable first Test hundred against England with his 12th four, another firm drive through extra-cover, and the lead was well past 300 when he attempted to hook Dilley, missed, and paid the penalty for not wearing a helmet by taking the ball just above his left eye. He was carried off and had to have four stitches in the wound.

Lillee's brave effort finally ended after 133 minutes in the middle when he edged Dilley to gully and so made possible the memorable line in the scorebook: Lillee caught Willey bowled Dilley 19.

Border returned but finally mishooked to give Willis a

wicket, and Botham finished off the innings by bowling Thomson leg-stump to collect his eleventh victim of the match. It was another remarkable demonstration of Botham's leonine strength and his great skill at constantly varying his fast-medium repertoire.

England were left with 354 to win in a little under seven hours batting. A draw or an Australian win seemed much more likely results, however, and the latter possibility grew stronger when in the twenty minutes' batting which England had before bad light stopped play for the day Randall badly misjudged a straight ball from Dymock, thrusting his front pad out and falling l.b.w. He departed, bitterly disappointed at having suffered a double failure on the ground where he had made 180 for North Perth before the tour began.

When the final day began Australia needed nine more wickets, England 335 more runs. There were five hours and twenty overs remaining in what had been an exceptionally tough Test match. The first hour made tense enough watching from any standpoint but it must have been agonising for those in the England dressing-room. Australia took two wickets to keep their sights firmly set on victory, and only the fact that Boycott batted through the hour with unhurried calm and relative comfort gave England any serious hope of surviving.

The green patches which had been evident on the pitch from the start of the match were still allowing generous movement for Lillee and Dymock as they began the attack. It was Dymock from the Grandstand end who broke through, dismissing Willey in exactly the same way that he had taken Randall's wicket the previous evening. Gower therefore found himself at the wicket for only the second over of the morning, facing a searching test of his technique. His temperament, of course, was not in question but he looked uneasy in a situation where he had to bat for as long as possible. That he lasted for fifty minutes was due partly to the fielders' generosity, because he gave hard slip chances to Wiener off Lillee and to Border off Dymock before chipping Dymock off his legs straight to mid-wicket.

Miller did his best during an uneasy twenty-minute sojourn in the middle but never looked like an England number five. How could he when he is a Derbyshire number six? He played at a lifting delivery from Thomson which he could probably have safely left alone and Chappell took a low catch at first slip with his usual dexterity. I cannot recall any slip fielder dropping so few catches as Greg Chappell.

Australia now ran into rather sterner resistance. Botham was six not out at lunch and, after surviving a slice past gully's left hand off Lillee, seemed to be playing with some command when he threw his wicket away in a flamboyant attempt to hook, or hoik, a ball pitched not very short and outside his off-stump. A very thin edge to Marsh resulted.

Brearley would obviously make no such scatter-brained strokes and after being beaten by a snorting delivery from Lillee first ball he settled in comfortably enough for just under half an hour on a beautiful, clear, sunny, breezy afternoon. There was no chance to sit back and enjoy the weather, however. Every ball was a severe test on the nerves – at least when it was bowled to anyone except Boycott, whose judgement was flawless. His technique has seldom looked more perfect.

Brearley's dismissal was unusual. Bright, revelling in the chance to bowl attackingly after all the limited-over cricket, and able moreover to do so to attacking fields with the pitch offering him just a little turn, drew Brearley forward and won a not very confident appeal for a catch behind the wicket.

Taylor, like Boycott and Brearley, had the right mental attitude for a backs-to-the-wall fight, and he lasted for fifty minutes. Just before tea Bright was joined in the attack by Wiener, who bustled through the overs in order to hasten the advent of the second new ball. At tea England were 178 for six, Boycott 83 not out, Taylor 11 not out, and 67 overs had been bowled. In the first over after the interval Taylor was bowled off his body as he tried to avoid playing a ball from Lillee which leapt back at him, and that seemed to be that.

It was asking too much of Dilley to bat for the best part of two hours after his first-innings heroics. Wasn't it? He defended sensibly again, however, as Lillee gave way again to Wiener so that the new ball could be taken sooner. Bright appealed most confidently for a catch behind as he finally spun one past Boycott's apparently impregnable defence. Marsh had whipped off the bails as well and the Australians looked in vain at both umpires.

Australia managed in the end to get four overs with the new

ball before the start of the mandatory twenty overs, and amidst wild excitement it was Geoff Dymock, that most gentlemanly and deserving of cricketers, who made the final decisive break and took the last three wickets in a sudden flourish.

Dymock has always been an exemplary bowler, a great trier who never resorts to histrionics, and his six for 34 confirmed that his success in India had been well-deserved. The chief individual heroes for Australia in this match – Hughes, Border and Dymock – were all men from the non-World Series Cricket team, although Lillee's all-round contribution had been vital to the eventual victory. Sadly, it was only Lillee's boorish performance on the second day which had spoiled a gripping Test match – this, and from an English point of view, the inadequacy of the batting. Randall, Willey, Gower and Botham all got themselves out with very bad batting misjudgements, and Miller's dismissal in both innings showed him to be a flimsy defender against high-class fast bowling – at least on a pitch such as this one was.

Brearley, defeated only for the second time in 24 Tests as captain, accepted the setback graciously, as he had at Melbourne the previous year. The pitches for the next two matches were likely to suit his team better, so there was no cause for mourning, only for disappointment. He was not to know then that the Sydney pitch would turn out to be wet rather than dry, depriving England of a chance to exploit their spinning superiority.

For Australia it was a time to rejoice. The victory came at an important time for the team and for the Board, just before the Christmas cricket rush. Big crowds were likely now for the next two Tests. The sudden success was personified in Greg Chappell, a man who since his early days in the game has disciplined himself to keep his emotions hidden behind a cool, dignified and often expressionless mask. Before this game he looked pale and weighed down by the responsibility of his job and the latent rumblings of the uneasy aftermath of the Packer war. When the last wicket fell he was the very picture of unrestrained joy, embracing his colleagues, his face full of colour again and beaming with a pleasure which did not need to be held back.

Chapter Six

ACB SHAME AND WEST INDIAN HONOUR

Australia's cricketing Christmas consisted of three more limited-over internationals and, in twelve hectic days between 29 December and 9 January, ten days of Test cricket. All but one of these games involved the home team.

There was some seasonal joy for each of the three sides before the Test rivalry was renewed, Australia coming from behind to beat the West Indies at Sydney, England suffering their first limited-over defeat against the West Indies at Brisbane and then winning their Boxing Day trial of strength with Australia.

So unexpected was Australia's win against the West Indies, who had dominated most of the game, that one heard familiar whispers about matches being purposefully thrown. Such rumours had been quite widespread in the two years of World Series Cricket, but on this occasion there can be no doubt that the West Indian collapse was entirely genuine.

The game, played four days before Christmas, was won by Australia by seven runs after they had started dismally, losing four wickets for 44 and five for 94 and being well below a realistic scoring rate until Ian Chappell, controversially restored to the Australian team despite his misdemeanours, came in to dominate the West Indies bowling. With coolness and resource he hit some cleanly struck blows in front of the wicket on either side, moving his feet quickly to give himself room to play the ball into the open spaces and making 63 not out in Australia's barely adequate 50-over total of 176 for six.

The West Indies were 111 for two, up with the not very demanding run-rate and apparently cruising to victory, when Richards fell for 62 to a casual shot off Dymock. Lloyd was caught off the next ball and suddenly Australia had a chance. Of the remaining batsmen only Kallicharran and Murray got into double figures and with Pascoe and Lillee firing the final volleys and Hogg recovering from an early mauling by Richards and Greenidge to bowl a fast, accurate spell, Australia scrambled home amidst wild excitement.

The game in Brisbane two days later did not match this one for tension, but as a cricket spectacular it seemed to satisfy the remarkably large crowd of 11,294 who had come to the Gabba on a sweltering Sunday afternoon to watch two 'alien' elevens. 'People will pay to see the best' was one of Kerry Packer's earliest assertions and on this occasion he was proved correct.

England's first one-day reverse may have had something to do with the fact that they lost the toss, for such life and bounce as there was in the pitch early in the game soon disappeared. It had more to do, however, with a continuation of the less-than-perfect fielding England had put on display at Perth. One had got used to something very near perfection in the Brearley era, and his team was clearly vulnerable whenever their high standards slipped.

On the face of it England made a useful score – 217 for eight from 50 overs – especially after losing a wicket to the first ball of the match, Randall pushing tentatively forward and edging Roberts to first slip. But Boycott and Willey renewed their profitable partnership, using the pace of the pitch and the outfield to push the score along after Boycott had been dropped by Greenidge off Roberts when he had made only 6. He went on to reach his third one-day fifty in a row off 91 balls, and when Willey was beaten by a good throw from King after contributing 34 off 51 balls, Gower played a succession of beautifully timed drives, pulls and forces through cover off the back foot. He and Boycott added 97 in 20 overs but after Gower had sliced a catch to deep third-man (he had twice escaped other more difficult chances) and Boycott had been fourth out for 68 in the 41st over, England failed to make the most of the final dash for runs. Roberts bowled especially straight and well, and a massive straight-driven six by Gooch off Holding was the only memorable blow struck by the later batsmen.

A rate of 4.34 on a pitch which had become a batting paradise was unlikely to be sufficient unless England took early wickets or West Indies had another day of panics. Neither of these happened. Haynes was dropped by Randall at square-leg off Willis and, when he hit Gooch to Underwood at mid-on after an opening stand of 109 with Greenidge, Richards soon proclaimed his royal blood to an appreciative crowd. He hit two of his first three balls for four, both off Gooch and both struck to his beloved mid-wicket with pulverising force. England's last real chance went when Bairstow got his right glove to a bottom edge as Richards hooked at Dilley but could not quite cling on. Richards was merely galvanised into greater action, first off-driving Underwood for four, then on-driving him for six. He reached 50 off 44 balls and Greenidge, already in the sixties when Richards had come in, was able almost to sit back and admire. He himself hit a six to demonstrate that in this mood there is no stopping the West Indies. They had four overs and one ball to spare when they won a match which kept the competition wide open.

Within two more days, however, England had virtually booked their passage into the finals. The Christmas Day celebrations at their Sydney hotel included a press party during which some highly effective sneezing powder was successfully counteracted by excellent Australian champagne. The home-produced wines are amongst the greatest joys of a trip to Australia. No doubt plenty was imbibed during the team's fancy-dress lunch, although the winner of the competition was one of the teetotallers, Bernard Thomas, who went as Rasputin. Ian Botham, busy growing a beard, lost some of his allure as a result in his portrayal of a female 'punk'.

Geoff Miller, who had been mainly responsible with John Lever for the Christmas celebrations, had arrived in Sydney late after an X-ray had suggested that his back condition would require prolonged treatment. He was immediately, if reluctantly, ruled out of contention for the remainder of the tour, and John Emburey, one of the official tour reserves and playing cricket in Melbourne at the time, was sent for as his replacement. England were extremely lucky to be able to make this direct swap: Emburey, a much-improved batsman, was not yet in Miller's class in that department but he is a superior close fielder and arguably a better off-spinner. Having taken 11 of his 19 Test wickets the previous winter in the two Tests at Sydney he had a great opportunity to go straight into England's Test team, and a good match in Brisbane after Christmas strengthened his claims.

David Bairstow also had to take a personal worry into the

The Perth Test was a well-balanced match until England's second-innings failure.
Above Laird becomes the first of 11 victims in the match for Botham; Brearley
and Taylor yell for l.b.w. as the ball cuts back from the off. *Below left* The
unassuming schoolmaster, Geoff Dymock, dismisses Willey l.b.w. (playing no
stroke) at Perth. *Below right* Dennis Lillee captures the wicket of Brearley,
caught by Marsh at Perth – Lillee's 100th in Tests against England.

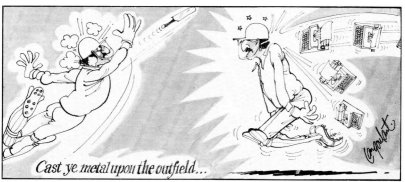

Cast ye metal upon the outfield...

The infamous aluminium bat incident. At the time one had to pinch oneself that it was really happening in a Test match. The umpires are Max O'Connell (glasses) and the inexperienced Don Weser. Langoulant's cartoon in the *Perth Daily News* sums up the press reaction (Australian writers were almost as critical as English ones) but Lillee ended up laughing all the way to the bank. The final action picture shows the end of Lillee's innings, caught by Taylor off the edge of his wooden bat – but Lillee's defiant second innings of 19 greatly contributed to Australia's victory.

Viv Richards was voted 'cricketer of the season' by a panel of experts. The command and virtuosity of his batting were breathtaking, and despite his serious injury he averaged 96 in the Tests and 109 in the One-Day Internationals. Here he hooks Lillee and straight-drives Dymock for boundaries in his dazzling 76 on the first morning of the Adelaide Test.

Boxing Day International, having heard that his father was ill, but he again played a valuable role as England put their two recent defeats behind them and won the noisiest game of cricket I can remember. Australia won the toss and batted on a pitch with a good deal more green in it than had been the case in the earlier matches. Botham bowled an ideal opening spell and after ten overs Australia were a mere 21 for two; a fourth-wicket stand of 59 by Greg Chappell and Hughes improved Australia's position and Ian Chappell came in to a warm reception from the crowd of 21,290 to score a brilliant 60 not out off only 50 balls. Willis stirred himself to give him a fiery baptism but successive fours off Underwood to square-leg and extra-cover and another two in a row off Gooch signalled the start of a cool assault on the England bowlers. So cool, in fact, that Chappell was able to find time to abuse Botham whenever he came into range. When he was joined by Lillee late in the innings Chappell motioned for Bairstow to go back to the boundary as Brearley set his naturally defensive field a little deeper. This was a fair joke, perhaps, but then Lillee joined in the fun, twice mocking Brearley when he failed to take relatively simple chances to run him out. With exaggerated gestures Lillee demonstrated to Brearley where the stumps were, how to throw and how to catch. On television Richie Benaud described this as 'kindergarten behaviour', although he was quickly interrupted by an advertisement. On radio Bobby Simpson said he thought it was all 'in very poor taste'. Brearley just shrugged his shoulders and a fiercely partisan crowd roared its approval. Brearley was being booed by crowds wherever he went (more than any captain since Jardine?) and one reason was that England, at this stage, continued to be inconvenient enough to win some matches!

That they did so on this occasion was again due to a marvellously composed and authoritative innings by Geoff Boycott. Graham Gooch had been reinstated as his opening partner in place of the hapless Randall and gave the innings a positive start, taking seven off Lillee's first over in which Boycott edged a ball at catchable height between Marsh and Greg Chappell. He was to give no more chances. Marsh missed another hard chance off Pascoe when Gooch was 14 and England had reached 41 when Gooch was l.b.w. to Hogg for 29 in the eleventh over.

This brought together those old friends Willey and Boycott, and to the accompaniment of a cacophony which would have made Melbourne, Calcutta or Port-of-Spain sound peaceful, they put on 111. It was not so much the crowd who raised the decibels as the activities at the nearby Sydney Showground. First there were speedway bikes revving over the loudspeakers, and then there was a spectacular firework display with some deafening bangs. All this seemed to increase the cool dignity with which Boycott placed the Australian bowling wherever he pleased, driving, deflecting and in the later stages even hooking with massive authority.

Willey once more struck with tremendous force on the offside and when Pascoe knocked back his off-stump in the 36th over England were as good as home. They did their best, however, to frighten their supporters. It can never be easy coming out to bat under the lights when quick runs are demanded and the white ball has lost its early gloss, and this, of course, was the first time that England had been obliged to bat under the lights in a match as opposed to a practice session. Gower, Randall, Botham and Brearley soon emerged blinking on the bright arena, only to disappear into the dark shadow of the pavilion a few minutes later. But Boycott continued to score at a satisfactory pace and 179 for six was the extent of England's decline. Bairstow joined his former county captain and helped him to get the 16 runs still needed. England won with eleven balls to spare and Boycott walked in bare-headed, arms aloft, 86 not out, another triumph behind him.

The first of the two Melbourne Tests was preceded by an extraordinary Press conference given by the chairman of the Australian Cricket Board, Bob Parish, on the day before the game, in the panelled boardroom of the Victorian Cricket Association. A wide array of journalists gathered to hear what punishment the Board, after their belated meeting on the affair of the aluminium bat, had decided to hand out to Dennis Lillee.

Mr Parish began by expressing surprise that there was so much interest in the matter. This in itself was the statement of someone either wilfully or genuinely blind to the significance of Lillee's defiance of the umpires and his captain. What followed confirmed this impression. A brief statement was read out which said that the Board had 'severely reprimanded' Lillee for his behaviour. No suspension, no fine. One's immediate reaction was that Lillee was too valuable both to the finances of Australian cricket and to its on-the-field success for him to be treated as he should have been. Instead of the game being proved bigger than the player, the reverse was now true.

Mr Parish's answers to some sharp questioning strengthened the view that the Board had acted pusillanimously and irresponsibly, ignoring the wider interest of the game, the conduct of which was still, officially, in their charge. The chairman said that the umpires reported no dissenting against their decision by Lillee, who, one understands, had been careful not to upset them by swearing, which at least was to his credit. No doubt, the matter being so unusual, he had a right to discuss the legality of the bat and whether or not it was damaging the ball. But he had no right to argue at such length, or to storm off the field of his own accord when a replacement bat was available, or to emerge several minutes later with the same aluminium bat which he had been told to change, or to brush past the umpires so that they were obliged to walk up to repeat their order, or to hurl the bat away in fury when his captain's will finally prevailed after a ten-minute hiatus: if all this did not amount to dissent, what did it amount to? Mr Parish had no satisfactory answer except to make the absurd implication that the Board were powerless to act on the most dramatic moment of the affair, the bat-throwing, because the umpires had not seen and therefore had not reported it. Yet one of the Board members, the chairman of selectors Phil Ridings, had seen the whole incident and so had 14,000 people on the ground and millions more on television. Many young cricketers who saw Lillee go effectively unpunished for his open defiance might well have got the impression that rebellious behaviour is part of the game. The thirteen Board members who had not been present at Perth (all but Mr Ridings) had not asked to see any video film of the incident. Had they done so they would surely have observed the dissent. The Board were thereby passing the buck to those unfortunate men in the middle – the umpires. It is true that Max O'Connell and Don Weser ought to have been firmer with

Lillee at the time, telling him that in their view the bat was damaging the ball and that he must either use one of the wooden replacement bats which had been brought out or retire and let the next batsman come in instead. But there was no doubt about who was being weak now. Mr Parish denied that the Board was afraid of Lillee taking legal action. As one heard the chairman's calm and sometimes evasive responses to the pertinent questions, one saw more clearly why the Australian players of the pre-Packer era had foundered against the stubborn official rock and how it had been possible for Mr Packer to exploit their frustrations in order to break down the barriers himself.

The Melbourne Test began in very hot weather on 29 December and after a promising first session for Australia it was the West Indies who emerged from the first day in a position of command.

Proceedings began with Australia making two changes to the side which had beaten England at Perth, Jim Higgs replacing Ray Bright and Rodney Hogg returning for Jeff Thomson, who was still injured. The West Indies ignored advice to include their only specialist spinner, Derek Parry, on a pitch widely expected to turn, and stuck to their four-man fast attack, Clive Lloyd returning, after his successful knee operation, in place of Collis King.

Lloyd called wrongly when Chappell tossed the coin in front of the cameras and Chappell, having condemned the pitch in advance as being too full of moisture and yet unlikely to last five days, chose to take a chance with the moisture in the hope that the pitch would become more difficult as the match went on.

At lunchtime Chappell could feel happy with his decision because the West Indian fast bowlers were desperately wayward and the breaks went the way of the home side. Wiener was dropped off Roberts when he was 16 and survived several confident early appeals in the first few overs but stayed to bat with solid, upright rectitude. Laird, edging a lifting delivery to first slip, was the only casualty before lunch, but he had stuck it out gamely for 69 minutes, seeing much of the shine off the ball.

Australia, beginning the afternoon at 68 for one, had reason to be optimistic, but in less than three hours playing time they were all out. Joel Garner, making up for what he lacked in sheer pace by greater accuracy and nastier lift than that achieved by Holding, Roberts and Croft, had bowled much the most testingly before lunch and he now took three wickets. Wiener was l.b.w. trying to hook a ball which kept low after adding a single to his lunch score. Chappell and Border then went through a torrid time. Chappell survived a vehement l.b.w. appeal from Garner to the third ball he received. Garner walked all the way up the pitch and stood at point for a time to let everyone know his feelings, then went desperately slowly back to his mark to deliver the next ball. Lloyd ought to have told Garner to get on with the game. Instead it was Chappell who made the point with telling effect by drawing back to adjust his gloves just as Garner finally started his run-up.

Garner calmed himself and continued to bowl well, making the ball lift waspishly off a pitch which was hardly adequate for a Test. Border watched his captain being hit in the ribs and the stomach, then receive a wicked bouncer from Holding which flew past his nose and over Murray's head for four byes. Border was out when he sparred at a lifting ball and sliced it to third slip and Chappell, finally softened up, tried belatedly to hook another lifting delivery and edged a gentle catch behind the wicket.

There was no Australian recovery this time. Hughes was caught at fourth slip trying to force off the back foot. Marsh, having also received a couple of blows, pushed a catch to short cover. Toohey hit one or two wristy drives, then perished to a ghastly slash to extra-cover, and it was left to Lillee and Hogg to make a few brave blows before the whole house collapsed. Holding and Croft had bowled far better after lunch. Had they been as accurate before, Australia might not have scored 100.

The West Indies batsmen, however, were to cover up their bowlers' early shortcomings by immediately demonstrating their brilliance. Greenidge, steadily putting behind him his disappointments on the 1975-76 tour of Australia, took two fours off Lillee's opening over and Haynes, with a burst of youthful belligerence, hit three boundaries off Hogg's first over at the northern end. For Hogg it was the start of a short but very unpleasant nightmare. 25 runs came off the first two overs and the two exuberant Bajans continued to savage anything not perfectly directed until Haynes was caught at second slip driving at an outswinger from Lillee.

The remainder of the day was notable for yet another peerless performance by Richards, who seemed almost to toy with the bowling for much of the time, and for a fine piece of sportsmanship by Greg Chappell, who immediately signalled 'no catch' when Greenidge edged a ball to Border at third slip. Border took the ball on the half-volley and umpire Crafter gave Greenidge out after consulting his colleague Mick Harvey at square-leg. But Border and Chappell saw justice done. The West Indies were 103 for one at the close, Richards 45 not out after another brilliant display. He once survived a very confident l.b.w. appeal by Dymock and was hit in the mouth by a ball from Hogg which brushed off his arm, but he hooked the next ball for six and otherwise peppered the extra-cover and mid-wicket boundaries with glorious strokes. Even on this unpredictable pitch he batted with supreme ease and without a helmet.

The temperature was again around 100° on the Sunday morning with a hot northerly breeze making life unpleasant for everyone and keeping the crowd down to 24,586 at its peak. In the early stages, however, there were no more than two-thirds of that number in the ground and they were strangely, almost eerily quiet as Dymock began the attack from the southern end.

Richards played from the start with such languid ease that he might have been batting against schoolboys. He off-drove Dymock's first ball and on-drove the second. Within a few minutes he had reached 50 off only 40 balls, and Greenidge, although determined to act as anchor-man, also allowed himself the luxury of two glorious off-driven fours against Lillee. The one-time tearaway bowled within himself from the start, striving for accuracy and achieving it. On a luckier day he might have had Richards caught when the ball flew off the shoulder of the bat past gully, and Richards also spooned Dymock back over mid-on when he tried to drive on the up. But Hogg was again given rough treatment by Richards and bowled only two overs before retiring to the pavilion for the day with back trouble. In six overs he had conceded 59 runs.

The fact that the ball was 'stopping' made driving hazardous except against the genuine half-volley, and both Greenidge and Richards were eventually out to the accurate Dymock when they mishit intended drives. Neither had been so fluent from the moment that Higgs was introduced into the attack from the southern end after the sweltering first hour. Although Kallicharran took four boundaries off the leg-spinner before lunch he did not always look at ease against him, and the same was true of Rowe when these two came together at the fall of Richards for 96 just before lunch.

Higgs got the first break after the interval, Kallicharran turning a leg-break into short-leg's hands, but it was Lillee, bowling a remorseless line and length off his short run, who eventually got through Rowe's defences after he had played patiently for 26 in 64 minutes at the crease.

A 'cool change' brought with it a sharp shower in mid-afternoon when the West Indies were 120 ahead with four wickets left and the captain and vice-captain, Lloyd and Murray, were together in the middle, both clearly determined to bat for as long as possible on this pitch which no one trusted.

Play was held up for 55 minutes but Lloyd and Murray had moved the total past 300 when the new ball was taken by Chappell at the first opportunity. Because of Hogg's injury, the captain was still gravely handicapped by having only three front-line bowlers and throughout the innings he used himself remarkably sparingly. The reliable Dymock eased his problems now by bowling Murray with his dangerous inswinger and then having Lloyd skilfully taken by Marsh off the inside edge as he drove; but the West Indies ended the day impregnably placed at 336 for seven, already 180 runs ahead with the pitch looking if anything less reliable as time passed.

Melbourne's weather never ceases to amaze and, at least for those watching under cover of the draughty Northern Stand, with a chilly southerly wind blowing in moist gusts, the Monday temperature was fifty per cent lower than it had been a mere eighteen hours earlier. Henry Blofeld and I sat shivering as we described the first two hours of play to late-bedders in Britain and the last hour to the early risers. This was the first time the BBC had sent ball-by-ball descriptions to Britain in a series not involving an England team.

From a strictly cricketing point of view it was a relatively prosaic day, during which the West Indies moved several inexorable steps closer to their first Test win at Melbourne.

Play began in a light drizzle which continued for much of the day, but due to the good sense of the umpires, Crafter and Harvey, only the last 37 minutes were lost. Far too often Test cricket has been held up in England in recent years because of gentle rain or bad light when conditions have been perfectly safe to play in. Genuine danger to batsmen and fielders should be the only reason for play to cease; there is nothing more likely to drive spectators away from Test cricket than for expensive tickets to be bought in advance only for the weather – perhaps unnecessarily – to ruin everyone's fun.

This miserable drizzly day began with a splendid old-fashioned tail-enders' stand. Andy Roberts enjoyed his finest hour as a Test batsman, although he had proved his ability on other occasions, once denying MCC a victory in the first match of a tour of the Caribbean and, at Edgbaston in the Prudential Cup of 1975, saving a match against Pakistan which enabled West Indies eventually to go on to win the World Cup. The task of Roberts and Garner was made much more comfortable by Dennis Lillee's surely mistaken decision to bowl off his short run at half-pace without letting fly in hope of quick wickets at the start. Perhaps he was saving himself for England. Nor did Dymock cause either batsman much trouble as ten runs were plundered from his first over. In three-quarters of an hour 64 runs had been added before Garner, having played one thoroughbred square-cut, miscued a sweep off Higgs. Roberts reached his first Test 50, his more memorable blows including an authentic hook for four off Lillee and some strong legside heaves off Higgs.

When Australia at last began their second innings, fifty minutes before lunch on the second day, the deficit they faced was 241. This was greater than the one they had surmounted in Brisbane, but the pitch here was altogether more venomous. Perhaps *insidious* would be a better word, for it was the occasional ball that kept low or lifted sharply which prevented batsmen from playing with confidence, especially against the fearsome quartet of West Indies fast bowlers, none of whom thought twice about banging the ball in short, not occasionally to test the batsman's nerve, but frequently to wear down his resolve.

One man, Bruce Laird, the smallest member of the side, took a very long time to crack, but the rest of the Australian house crumbled steadily before the hammer blows of the four-man demolition squad. Clive Lloyd set attacking fields throughout and patiently awaited the inevitable. Between lunch and tea Wiener's determined defence was ended by a lifting ball from Croft, and Border, who had been missed at second slip off Garner when he had made only two, was l.b.w. to a ball from Holding which came back and kept low. Chappell played some fine shots after tea but did not seem to have the stomach on this pitch for a long and gutsy struggle of the kind that Laird was waging so bravely. Making no fuss about a horrid blow on his left hand, Laird reached fifty off the first ball after tea, but lost his captain, caught off the glove as he hooked at Roberts, and then saw Hughes dropped at fourth slip off Holding when only six. Hughes survived to take Australia into the new year with a series of sparkling strokes but with no serious hope of saving the game.

The first day of 1980 dawned cool but bright with Australia's total standing at 167 for three, still 67 runs behind. Laird, 63 not out overnight, received a pain-killing injection in his injured hand at the end of the first over and not surprisingly fell to a catch in the gully only two overs later. Poor Toohey, doomed to lose his Test place to Ian Chappell, who had just been added to the squad for the next game against England, lasted less than half an hour before he edged a good delivery from Croft to the wicket-keeper and it was left to Hughes, with some delightfully crisp strokes, to show that the remorseless West Indian fast bowlers were not quite invincible. He had doubled his overnight 33 when he was missed at deep fine-leg from a hook off Roberts, but a few balls later Roberts had him l.b.w. and only the tail remained.

Marsh was bowled round his legs by Croft, Roberts pitched short to Lillee and took a simple catch off his own bowling (England's bowlers had seemed reluctant to pitch short at Lillee in Perth early in his crucial innings), and Garner took the last two wickets after lunch.

Greenidge and Haynes, having taken 25 off the first two overs in the first innings, took seven overs and two balls to knock off the 19 runs required for the first-ever West Indies Test win at Melbourne. Remarkably enough it was only their sixth win in any Test in Australia on six tours and, this being only a three-match series, they at least could not now lose, as they had in all previous series in the Antipodes. Such was the superiority of their fast bowlers over Australian batsmen that there seemed no reason other than the physical breakdown of one or more of these men that they should not go on to beat Australia again, or to overcome England when they met them away and at home during 1980-81. For Clive Lloyd (himself now moving more freely after his knee operation than he had for some years) and his team of formidable talents it was indeed a happy new year.

This could not be said for the Australian Cricket Board, who began the match under fire for their weakness on the Lillee affair and ended it mourning the worst crowd attendance for a Melbourne Test in the Christmas/New Year period for many years. Only 89,045 people attended the four days' cricket, compared with 128,758 for England's 4-day match the previous year and 222,755 for the equivalent West Indies Test in 1975-76 which also ended in four days. The actual amount of dollars taken at the gate, due to inflation, was only a little down, but the Melbourne public had spoken. 'We don't like the new programme,' they seemed to have said, 'and we certainly don't like a losing Australian team.'

Chapter Seven

THE MYSTERY OF THE UNCOVERED PITCH

England selectors can seldom have agonised as long over the selection of a Test team as they did before the vital second Test which began in Sydney at 3.30 on a muggy January afternoon.

During the Melbourne Test England had comfortably defeated Queensland in a four-day game at Brisbane, and two of the major successes in this match, Graham Gooch, who made 115 and 53, and John Emburey, who had been called from club cricket for St Kilda to take the place of the unfortunate Geoff Miller and who not only took six wickets in Brisbane but also scored 50, were named in the twelve. All those who played at Perth with the exception of Miller retained their places and, in the end, Emburey was omitted, although not until ten minutes before the belated start did England make their decision to play six specialist batsmen, with Willey entrusted to share the spinning duties with Underwood. Lever was left out on a split vote of the five selectors in conditions which would have suited him perfectly and Boycott, who had a stiff neck, only played under strong pressure.

One reason, perhaps, for Boycott's reluctance and for everyone's anxiety was the state of the pitch which had been left uncovered during a heavy downpour in the early hours of the new year. One does not envy groundsmen their job in preparing suitable Test pitches when the weather can foil the best-laid plans, but to have left the pitch uncovered three nights before the game was at best an unwise gamble and at the worst sheer negligence. When it finally stopped raining on the afternoon before the match began, the pitch was revealed as muddy, mottled and underprepared. It rained again on the Friday morning and umpires Bailhache and Copeland waited for a long time for damp patches on the square to dry out. So dry had the weather been in the weeks leading up to the Test that the process did not last long and they were unquestionably right in starting the game when they did. But it was clear from the abundance of green patches that whichever side won the toss must field first and enjoy themselves. Brearley called wrongly.

At Perth the England captain had joined the long list of those who had put the opposition in and lost a Test match, but this is always a dubious statistic – captains often bat first and lose too! – and Greg Chappell (who had been reluctant to start play) did not hesitate for a second to put England in. Everything was going for his side in this situation: not only the green, damp pitch, but also a muggy atmosphere and the psychological pressure which had built up after the long and anxious wait for the umpires to decide when play would begin. In England in these circumstances there would have been three and a half hours' play because of the rule permitting an extra hour when one has been lost to the weather. For the bowlers a two-and-a-half-hour session in these conditions was ideal, and it meant that, if England were to be hustled out quickly, only a declaration could have got Australia in to bat that evening in similarly difficult circumstances.

Australia certainly seized the chance well. Lillee's first over was harmless enough, and carefully negotiated by Gooch, but Dymock at once had Boycott in difficulties, dipping his very first ball into the pads and yelling for l.b.w. Boycott took eight runs from an on-drive and a leg-glance but the last ball of Dymock's second over he attempted to drive at full stretch, only to find the ball hanging out of reach and then dipping in to hit the off-stump.

Dymock was making the ball both cut away off the seam and swing in the air and the first over that he bowled to Randall, now back at number three, was one of those when the ball almost 'talked' for the bowler. Such swing and cut was hardly calculated to improve the confidence of a batsman who had made three ducks and only 44 runs in his last six innings. But it was Lillee, bowling at three-quarters of his full pace and allowing the pitch to do his work, who nailed the Nottingham Imp when a ball lifted in line with the off-stump and was edged to first slip.

Gooch and Willey continued the grim, unequal yet intensely interesting battle. Largely because of the long delay, only just over 7,000 people were in the ground but they had their money's worth in the two-and-a-half hours' play possible. At 31 they saw Willey contort his body as he tried to keep down another wicked delivery from Dymock which lifted and left him, but an edge and a fine catch by Wiener at fourth slip were the only results. Gooch, having been missed by Dymock at backward short-leg off a lifter from Pascoe, and having hit two delightful off-drives which would have been four on most days but which on the damp outfield were worth only three and two, succumbed for 13 in Lillee's second spell. After 87 minutes of worthy effort the finish of his innings was disappointing; he left an inswinger alone in the hope that it would bounce over the stumps, only to see the ball curve in and remove the off-bail as if it had been remote-controlled.

Brearley had come out at number five, two ahead of his official place in the order, padded up from head to foot but in no way shirking the crisis. He was booed and jeered to the crease. This was familiar to him but the taunting had an extra venom on this occasion, perhaps because Brearley had warned before the game that, if the crowd hooliganism evident in so many of the matches continued, a cricketer would be killed before long by some mindless drunk hurling a full can or a block of ice or even another metal staple such as the one which had struck Bob Taylor at a night match earlier in the season. Two hours after the close of play on this first day of the Test I shared a taxi from the ground to my hotel with a man in his fifties who was almost too drunk to walk, but certainly not to talk. His opening remark to me was: 'We got the rotten pommies today then.' His companion recognised my voice and was clearly embarrassed by his friend who, in the course of the brief journey, became a warm friend of mine too, assuring me that his wife would not be able to contain herself with envy that her husband should have shared a taxi with the famous BBC commentator Christopher Martish – Whatshisname! I was left wondering about this strange disease of pommy-hatred. But from a cricketing point of view the gentleman was right: Australia had England on the run.

Brearley battled it out for an hour, playing nothing he did not have to, but Gower succumbed meekly to a good delivery from Greg Chappell, which pitched on the leg-stump and hit the off as Gower aimed across the line in that loose-wristed way which looks so silky when he hits and so careless when he misses.

The only stand of any substance was provided by a mixture of Brearley's defence and Botham's attack. A couple of powerful legside swings by Botham, one a cleanly struck six over long-on off Chappell, were about all English supporters had to cheer during what for them was an afternoon of almost unmitigated disaster. Botham's brave effort to seize back some initiative from the bowlers ended when Pascoe gave him a brutish delivery which lifted sharply and flew off the top of the bat well over Greg Chappell's head at first slip. With superb timing and instantaneous reflexes Chappell caught the ball in both hands at full stretch with his feet off the ground.

74 for six became 75 for seven when Brearley lost patience and tried to loft Dymock over mid-wicket, succeeding only in slicing a catch to mid-on. But Taylor and Dilley held on until the close, when England were 90 for seven. Conditions had certainly been difficult, and Australia had bowled well, but this was no old-fashioned 'sticky' and better must have been hoped for, even by an England side bitterly disappointed to have lost the toss.

The tail decided on the Saturday that if it was going to wag it should do so with vigour. The bowlers were anxious to get at Australia before all the moisture left the pitch. Taylor was caught behind in Lillee's first over and Willis holed out off Dymock, Wiener judging an awkward catch well, but Dilley and Underwood hit with better luck, until Underwood's enjoyment was ended by a very good diving catch by Border.

Australia began their reply to England's 123 at 11.45 and must have felt pleased with their start as Wiener took advantage of some uncharacteristically wayward bowling by Botham to get some early runs quickly. Wiener's partner on this occasion was not Laird but McCosker, because Laird had not fully recovered from the bruised hand suffered against the West Indian fast bowlers earlier in the week.

Willis was given the new ball for the first time in a major match on the tour in preference to Dilley, and he took the first wicket in his third over when McCosker edged a ball of full length low to fourth slip where Gower took a good catch. Thereupon Ian Chappell re-entered the Test stage which he had left, disenchanted and discontented, in 1976. Less than a month before he had stated that if the Board had suspended him a second time for his exhibition in Adelaide he would have given up the game because, as he put it, 'I've had a gutsful.' But the suspension of the six-week sentence gave him the incentive to carry on on pain of good behaviour, and according to strict batting criteria he demanded his own recall by running at once into top form. He needed to be in form to survive on this pitch and Willis gave him a testing time early on, although, with Chappell going onto the back foot to almost everything, Willis could not hit the right length to disturb him consistently.

Underwood had come on for the fifth over, Wiener at once dancing down the pitch to attack and thereby succeeding, at least for a while, in preventing the expert from settling immediately into the loose-armed rhythm which normally enables him to put each delivery where he wants it. Chappell also looked to attack, and in particular to sweep, dangerous stroke though that is. However it has the advantage that if the bat misses, the pad usually comes to the rescue, and umpires in Australia practically never give a batsman out who sweeps and is hit on the front pad.

Chappell's initiation included a blow on the solar plexus from a ball by Willis, and this was followed by a dangerous attempt to square-cut an off-cutter which on a less fortunate day would certainly have resulted in an edge to the wicket-keeper. Freshly determined by this escape he hooked and cut Willis for fours and Australia appeared to be taking a grip when Wiener, facing an exploratory over from Willey before lunch, drove crisply to Brearley at mid-on. With a perfect pick-up and throw Brearley threw down the stumps at the bowler's end with Wiener still out of his ground. It was his second run-out in three Test matches and Messrs Wood and Darling, the kamikaze kids of the previous season, no doubt sent him a telegram.

On what was now a fresh and sunny afternoon the Chappell brothers took Australia to 71 for two, whereupon Australia collapsed and the domination of the bowlers was dramatically restored. Greg Chappell, subdued and uncertain, got an edge to a ball from Underwood which turned. Then Ian Chappell, now the key to a big score, earned the dubious honour of becoming Graham Gooch's second Test victim (Sunil Gavaskar was the first – nothing but the best for the Essex demon) by driving at a wide away-swinger and edging it to slip.

Nothing underlined the difficulties inherent in the pitch more than the success of Gooch, normally just an occasional purveyor of tidy medium-pace seamers in county cricket. Today he bowled like a man inspired, keeping an admirably full length and a resolute off-stump line. At the Randwick end Ian Botham, having been made to wait for once after the two poor overs he had delivered with the new ball, now produced another superb spell of swing bowling. Cutting the ball away late off the seam at a brisk pace, he looked almost unplayable. Incredible to relate, England's slip fielders dropped no fewer than five chances off Botham and Gooch, yet of the last six Australian batsmen only Hughes and Border (both dropped) reached double figures and four of them were caught behind the wicket. Marsh, driving to mid-off, and Higgs, bowled round his legs by Underwood attempting a sweep, were the exceptions. Pascoe made a spirited ten not out after he had been dropped off Dilley before he had scored, and this helped Australia to attain a lead of 22, which looked a good deal more significant when England lost three second-innings wickets in a disastrous final session on Saturday to take the total number of wickets to 23 in eight and a half hours.

England desperately needed a calm and solid opening stand from Boycott and Gooch, but in Dymock's very first over a ball cut away to take the edge of Gooch's bat and Greg Chappell claimed a low catch. Willey came in at 'first-drop' this time instead of Randall. It was Len Pascoe who restored Australian supremacy in a fine spell of hostile fast bowling, taking two vital wickets as many of Sydney's biggest crowd of the season (24,717) made their way to the exits, apparently glutted by the bowlers' feast. Willey was beaten by sheer pace. There is the slightest movement back of the right foot as he first moves into any stroke, and on this occasion he was a fraction late getting into line of a ball which knocked back his off-stump.

Boycott was batting with a skill and judgement greater than anyone on either side had so far managed when Pascoe got a ball to lift sharply and to lob off the top of the bat to gully. England were thus 29 for three or, in effect, seven for three. The intrepid Derek Underwood waddled out as nightwatchman to join Mike Brearley, who had come in at number four, and the last few anxious overs were somehow negotiated without further losses. It had been a breathtaking day, exciting and exhausting to watch.

The mayhem ended at last on the third day. By judicious and brave defence and some canny nudging and deflecting, the somewhat unlikely pair of Underwood and Brearley batted through the first hour and a half against the four seam bowlers. Chappell decided against gambling with the possibility of some quick runs off Higgs, who might nonetheless have been the man to rid Australia of the frustrating night-watchman.

Underwood has always been a cricketer of admirable character, by nature a 'bonny fighter'. In the first innings, when having a quick dip, he had looked disinclined to get into line against the fast bowlers but this time, although several times hit around the thigh and more than once above the waist, he resolutely got behind the ball, played with a straight bat and generally picked up runs a little more easily than his partner. Brearley's was a typical effort: staunch, brave, shrewd, limited. Although he made only 19 his innings of just under two hours in all was worth more than the sum on the board. Together with Underwood, he had stopped the headlong slide to destruction.

Randall was dancing down the pavilion steps well before Brearley had reached the pavilion and although he fidgeted as much as ever when he got to the crease he played with great discretion and determination. He was 11 not out at lunch when England were 104 for 4. They could hardly have hoped for much better and at one point, when Lillee made two wildly optimistic l.b.w. appeals, the frustration felt by Australia was very evident.

During a tense afternoon's cricket, however, the Australian bowlers again brought a fascinating match into balance. Underwood, caught at short-leg off Dymock in the first over after lunch, received a hero's welcome from another good crowd – and by good I mean not just substantial in size but also better behaved, less unpleasantly partisan and more appreciative of good cricket than the crowds who had watched the limited-over games. They had even applauded Brearley when he was out!

David Gower walked out to join Derek Randall knowing that

he was facing something of a personal crisis. England's hopes rested now on these two 'flair players', neither of whom had been in good form. When a batsman is out of form he is almost always out of luck as well. But in the course of a brilliant innings on this Sunday afternoon in Sydney, Gower had a good deal of luck. He gave only one actual chance (at 72) but frequently played and missed outside his off-stump, notably against Pascoe. In between, he middled the ball with ease, and he graced the day with a series of beautiful offside strokes off either foot and sometimes a powerful pull to mid-wicket.

Whilst Gower both sparkled and sparred, Randall played with skill and visible determination, letting nothing past his bat that he did not intend to. His fidgeting and procrastination roused Lillee to fury at one point but the outward demonstration of the needle between the two was a red herring. The game was developing its own inbuilt drama.

It was Greg Chappell, still getting his slow-medium seamers to deviate a little either way off a pitch which was gradually becoming more docile, who broke the useful sixth-wicket partnership of 51. Bowling round the wicket to Randall, he found the edge of the bat with a ball angled across the right-hander. Four overs later Chappell had an equally important wicket when he persuaded Botham, who had restrained himself for almost three overs, to open his shoulders and drive at a slightly slower ball. He did not get to the pitch and the ball flew hard in the air to extra-cover where Wiener clung on joyously.

At Botham's fall England's lead was only 152. Taylor, Dilley and Willis remained but everything now depended on Gower, 68 not out at tea when England were 189 for seven. The new ball was taken at the first opportunity (85 overs) and although Taylor stuck there doggedly for a time he was bowled by Lillee at 211 and Dymock removed Dilley at 218. It was now do or die for Gower (who was 82 when Willis, the last man, walked out) and with thrilling skill he hooked and square-cut Lillee for successive fours. In the next over he defied Chappell's defensive field with a feathery late-cut off a half-volley but, when two short of his hundred, he saw Willis fall to another very low catch by the Australian captain. From a distance, Willis seemed fully justified in awaiting the umpire's decision that the ball had not been scooped up on the half-volley.

The umpires were called upon for more difficult decisions when Australia, facing an unpleasant 40 minutes at the crease before the close of the third day, began their attempt to score 216 to win the match and the rubber. Wiener survived a confident appeal for a catch off the inside edge by Taylor off Willis, another for l.b.w. and then a hard chance, again off the inside edge, which Taylor just got a glove to as the ball whistled by for four. Thereafter Wiener played solidly but McCosker, going right back onto his stumps to a straight ball from Underwood, appeared fortunate to get the benefit of the umpire's doubt. McCosker believed he had got a thin inside edge. The fact was that both he and Wiener not only survived, but reduced the target to 191.

The rest day was cool and showery, though not wet enough to prevent the cricket journalists of Australia and England from engaging in a very sociable Test match of their own as guests of Benson and Hedges. Australia had in Bobby Simpson a player several classes ahead of anyone else, and his side duly won by five wickets a match notable for some controversial incidents. After Simpson had been given out 'handled the ball' and had hit his wicket down in 'fury' at the gamesmanship of the opposition, I was forced to protest when the Reuter correspondent Brian Williams struck a delivery of mine with an aluminium bat. I thought the bat was damaging the ball but Williams argued heatedly with the umpires before storming off to the pavilion and re-emerging several minutes later with the same bat. Eventually his captain, Michael Coward of the *Adelaide Advertiser*, had to come out and pacify his errant star player, who after a nine-minute delay agreed to go on with a willow bat after throwing the other one away. I had Williams stumped three balls later after he had failed to make contact with three huge flails of the willow and I would not be able in a respectable book to reveal what he said to me in the pavilion afterwards!

Perhaps the most amusing aspect of this re-enactment of recent notorious events was that the umpires, both first-graders, took a long time to realise that the players were not in earnest. There was a deeply concerned look on their faces as they asked if I really wished to go through with my protest.

Refreshed by the hospitality (as Henry Blofeld remarked, 80 per cent of their guests went home convinced that Benson and

Hedges made wine) we returned to the stern business of Test cricket. Australia's target – a further 191 when play began on a bright and breezy morning – was made much more accessible by the fact that the pitch had rolled out on the fourth morning into a flat, dead surface. The green patches had disappeared and the only help the England bowlers got all day was a little bit of turn for Derek Underwood.

The great spinner did his best, and the eventual result tells of none of the tension which kept another excellent crowd (21,461, making a total for the match of 74,504) guessing tensely at the outcome until mid-afternoon. Underwood dismissed Wiener in his third over, having opened the bowling with Dilley. Wiener played back to a faster ball and was bowled off the inside edge, deceived like many another inexperienced player by the zip off the pitch which Underwood, with his loose arm, can achieve.

An uneasy stand followed between Chappell the elder and McCosker, who obeyed few of the rules of foot movement against Dilley's sharp pace and who sliced a four just over Botham's head at second slip. Dilley hurried Chappell into a defensive stroke soon afterwards but the ball just missed the leg stump as it skimmed off the inside edge. Instead it was Underwood who snared Chappell, brilliantly caught low and left-handed by Botham off bat and pad at silly point.

Brother Greg began what was to be his matchwinning innings at 51 for two, at once batting with a good deal more confidence and conviction than he had shown in the first innings. As usual he acquired the majority of his early runs with strokes played off either foot between mid-wicket and mid-on in that upright, leaning style which is uniquely his. But although the pitch was now so tame Botham and Underwood were bowling an immaculate line and length and runs came slowly. McCosker gradually looked more convincing, sticking to his task with imperturbable dedication and Chappell seldom looked disturbed by his old tormenter Underwood, launching a sudden attack on him early in the afternoon with a beautifully timed swing to leg and a graceful off-drive.

There was one moment of unexpected comedy amidst all the tension when umpire Copeland lost his white panama, blown off by a sudden gust, and was forced to pursue the hat all the way to the boundary. Umpire Bailhache duly signalled four.

But Mr Bailhache had a much harder decision to make a little later and his verdict finally settled which way the game would go. McCosker was caught behind soon after lunch off a ball from Underwood which turned more sharply than any other and in the next over, with the total 100 and his own score 32, Chappell drove lazily at Dilley outside the off-stump. The ball very clearly deviated to the wicket-keeper and the England fielders went up in uproarious appeal. To their openly expressed amazement and indignation Chappell stood his ground and umpire Bailhache shook his head.

As Brearley later remarked: 'If Greg had been out Australia would have been 100 for four and a lot of pressure would have been put on the other batsmen. Obviously, from our reactions, we thought it was out.'

Chappell's comment was simply: 'England were convinced I touched it; I was sure I didn't. I am glad the umpire agreed with me.'

Following the decisions which had gone against them in the earliest phase of the Australian innings England were convinced that, as one player put it, they had been 'done'. It is certainly true that the gods had not exactly smiled on them in this match. What is not in doubt is that England's last chance had gone. An admirable stand of 105 between Chappell and Hughes now took Australia to the edge of victory. Although Botham and Gooch pinned both men down for a long period with steady medium-pace bowling, the runs came gradually in ones and twos until Chappell signified the final surge with a glorious off-drive against Gooch. Hughes went even better with a searing straight drive off Underwood. He survived another confident appeal for a bat/pad catch by Botham at leg-slip off Willey – the ball in fact apparently coming off his boot – but Australia were only 13 runs short of their target when he holed out to mid-on off Willis, who had been given little chance by his captain and who had surely deserved a few overs at the start of the day before he stiffened up and batsmen had a chance to get set.

Such theories were useless to England now. Chappell launched into Willey with three roasting legside fours in one over and he finally came within an ace of winning the match and reaching his hundred in the same shot. He needed six to do so and Botham obligingly gave him a slow long-hop to help him achieve it, but Chappell's lofted pull fell some fifteen yards short. Thanks to their captain's commanding batting at the end, Australia had won with some style.

Botham's gesture was a piece of old-fashioned sportsmanship which did him credit. Indeed the match as a whole had restored some faith that Test cricket would hold its own against the new wave in Australian cricket.

In the event the winning of the toss had proved more important at the end of the match than at the start. The pitch was almost as difficult to play on during the second day as it had been during the first, although the psychological factors at the start of England's innings had been very significant. By the fourth day a spiteful pitch had become an amiable one and Brearley was surely right in estimating that the side which won the toss had about a 60-40 chance of winning the match. Brearley felt the two sides were evenly balanced. Certainly England had every reason to feel aggrieved about the wet pitch at Sydney. They had always considered this the Test they were most likely to win because of their spinning superiority and the fact that most Sydney pitches become dry and dusty. This one, of course, never did.

Although Chappell claimed that, whatever might have been decreed at Lord's, Australia had regained the Ashes, there was no doubt in my mind that the TCCB's decision not to put them at stake had been justified by events. The preparation of both teams for a Test series had been inadequate and England now had only one more first-class game in three weeks before the final Test. In addition, such factors as luck with the toss and with umpiring decisions have a much greater chance of balancing out between two sides over a five-match rubber than over a three-match one. Moreover, the Anglo-Australian series inevitably lost some of its prestige by being parcelled up with a seemingly interminable one-day competition and the simultaneous series against the West Indies.

Chapter Eight

WEST INDIES – ONE-DAY WONDERS

Limited-over cricket had the stage to itself in the fortnight following the Sydney Test. England were certainly not complaining, although they had never hidden the fact that the Test matches were their priority and that their relative success in the one-day games, although an immense consolation, was only a limited balm to the deep wound of defeat in successive Tests against a team which, in Brearley's words, 'might be better than us, though I doubt it.'

The weather made certain of England's place in the final of the Benson and Hedges World Series Cup. Even by Melbourne standards (and Melbourne's standards are in my experience rivalled only by Manchester's), it rained very hard on the morning of Saturday, 12 January, and at the scheduled hour of starting, ten o'clock, there was water covering most of the outfield. From the abandoned match England and the West Indies both took a point and this meant that even if England lost their last three qualifying matches they could not be caught by Australia.

The most disappointed men in the England team were Wayne Larkins and John Emburey, who had been chosen ahead of Geoff Boycott (suffering from a stiff neck and a sore hand) and Derek Underwood. By his own exalted standards the latter had been disappointing and Emburey, an altogether fresher cricketer at the time, was a sound choice.

Larkins and Emburey got their chance two days later, along with two equally long-suffering reserves in John Lever and Graham Stevenson. Lever, whose first tour, to India, had been an instant success, had spent much of the previous tour of Australia on the sidelines, and it must have hit him especially hard this time to find himself a reserve after the injury to Mike Hendrick. In theory Lever ought as a result to have come back into the front line of England's attack, but the loyal Willis and the promising Dilley had been preferred, though Lever would have been suited well by the bowling conditions which England had faced in both the first two Tests. Lever took his disappointment without any outward sign of his despair. He spoke thus of his reactions:

'It's been hard, but I've had several chats with Bob Taylor and I don't feel quite so hard done by. He spent four tours as understudy to Knottie. You have to accept it. You have to keep fit. You have to keep bowling in the nets. But that's the hardest part. If a team is winning you know you haven't got much chance of getting in and it seems a waste of time. Other lads are in the same boat and we try to keep each other going, which is a big help . . . . When the game is on and I am not acting as 12th or 13th man I find I have to get away from the ground so I am not so depressed about not playing. It helps to get away to the beach and do some sun-bathing or play golf or a bit of squash. You must get away from the ground because that's where you can get very depressed about not playing. You don't feel a part of it. Time's gone very slowly this time, especially in the first three or four weeks. We had some funny games. Time really dragged before Christmas especially. I'm not one of those quick bowlers who like to have a rest. I like to keep playing.'

Graham Stevenson knew when he came out as Hendrick's replacement that he would be likely to get very little cricket, but he must have hoped for more than two games in seven weeks. He would have been working as a clerk in a power station if he had not received the call to join the team, and when he was selected to play for England against the Australians in his first major international match, the limited-over game at the Sydney Cricket Ground, on 14 January, he referred to it as a 'nice break in me 'oliday'. A good, solid, down-to-earth, rough-humoured Yorkshire lad without an ounce of pretension or conceit, Stevenson took his chance handsomely.

It was the last of the four limited-over meetings between England and Australia in the eliminating round of the competition, and Brearley decided to put the opposition in when he won the toss. In the event a brown, grassless, damp-looking pitch gave little support to any of the bowlers, but despite an opening stand of 74 in 23 overs between McCosker and Wiener

Australia collapsed dramatically, losing their last seven wickets for 15 runs, and only totalled 163. The three 'second-eleven' bowlers who had replaced Willis, Dilley and Underwood did well to a man. Lever bowled beautifully to return figures of two for 11 in nine overs; Emburey varied pace and trajectory most skilfully in taking two for 33 in ten overs (most of them delivered to the two best Australian batsmen, Greg Chappell and Hughes), and Stevenson, after a modest first spell, came back to whistle out four batsmen (including Lillee first ball) and to run out a fifth off his own bowling with a quick pick-up and throw which proved that, however slow-witted he may give the impression of being off the field, he is a fine, instinctive cricketer.

England ought by right to have won in comfort, but they chose a hair-suit, and however much one might feel that there was far too much limited-over cricket in this dizzy Australian season, one has to admit in retrospect that time and again the day-night matches at the SCG turned out to be thrilling and marvellously unpredictable. On this occasion Australia had collapsed so dismally against another superlative fielding performance by England (not a throw seemed to go anywhere except straight over the bails) that they really had no right to win. Yet a couple of hours after the supper break England themselves were in such a desperate position that they too appeared to have as much chance as an oyster on the walrus and the carpenter's beach.

Only Graham Gooch stood firm, indeed stood up and dominated the Australian bowling, driving Thomson through the covers for four in the first over and not looking back. But Dennis Lillee, urged on by a crowd of just over 12,000 and himself driving the crowd to further frenzies by the splendid hostility of his efforts, took four wickets for a mere 12 runs in an inspired spell of bowling from the Randwick end. By the 25th over England had been reduced by a combination of good bowling by Lillee and Greg Chappell and their own batting errors to a miserable score of 61 for six. Then the human tank, David Bairstow, marched out to play an innings which was both representative of his character and yet entirely out of character.

Normally Bairstow is a vigorous attacking batsman. This time he defended with tenacity whilst Gooch went on remorselessly gaining his runs, almost entirely from powerful drives. At 105, in the 39th over, he lofted one such stroke hard to extra-cover where McCosker dived to take a brilliant catch. From this apparently hopeless position the unlikely trio of Bairstow, Emburey and Stevenson guided England to a stunning victory with seven balls to spare. Emburey is not normally a strong striker of the ball and in the circumstances he played a gallant little innings of 18. Then the rugged strength of young Stevenson was put to effective use. Chappell had used up all the overs belonging to himself, Lillee and Pascoe and it was the Queensland pair of Dymock and, especially, Thomson, who suffered as Stevenson lofted stroke after stroke over or through the covers. Chappell, with his elder brother looking on from third-man, did little to plug the gaps and Thomson obligingly continued to bowl outside Stevenson's off-stump. Five years before – just five short years – Thomson had demoralised an England batting side which included John Edrich, Colin Cowdrey, Keith Fletcher, Dennis Amiss, Alan Knott and Tony Greig. Now he was being slogged at will by a tailender who had not yet played Test cricket. *C'est la vie d'un cricketeur!*

Stevenson hit the winning runs with a four to extra-cover, denying us even the agony of a tense final over. 22 runs had come off the last three overs and Stevenson had hit 28 off 18 balls. Bairstow, whose comment to Stevenson on his arrival at the crease had been 'We'll get these easy' (it had not occurred to anyone else that they would), had restricted himself admirably for 24 overs in making 21 not out. At one point his right arm had seized up in a painful muscle spasm. At the end he ran off, joyously patting his fellow tyke on the back and raising his arms aloft. One of my abiding memories of this tour will be of David Bairstow running off time and again into the Sydney floodlights, red hair aflame and his broad face creased in an open smile.

How ironical it was that England continued to do so well in the night matches, the WSC creation which they had only reluctantly accepted! As soon as England got back to daylight and a red ball, they lost. They played the West Indies two days later on a glorious summer's day at Adelaide and Clive Lloyd's team won by an overwhelming margin of 107 runs to close the door between Australia and the finals.

Brearley won the toss and more for negative reasons (the West Indies like to bat second in limited-over games) he put his opponents in. England were unchanged though Boycott had been selected in Randall's place, only to rule himself unfit because of a bruised hand. In the event he would have been unlikely to have done anything more than lessen the margin of defeat, because the score of 246 for five achieved by West Indies in their 50 overs was a bit too good, even on a perfect batting pitch. Greenidge with 50, Kallicharran with 57 and Richards with 88 hit the ball more or less where they wished. Emburey, Willey and Botham escaped, however, with tidy figures and Botham dismissed Kallicharran with a catch off his own bowling which bordered on the miraculous, leaping to his right to push up a hard-hit drive, then catching the rebound behind his head at full stretch in his left hand as he fell to the ground.

England's response was a sorry affair. Roberts bowled well to take five for 22 and the man of the match award of £250. King picked up four wickets, which was a happy return for an exuberant all-rounder who had only recently recovered from a painful bout of sinusitis. Only Gooch, Larkins, Botham and Bairstow reached 20, and none went on to play a big innings.

Understandably England's desire to win had been shallower than that of the West Indies team, and the same applied when the West Indies, now safely in the final, took on Australia for the final qualifying match at Sydney two days later. Australia, with McCosker making 95 and Lillee again bowling excellently, picked up £1,750 prize money and a little lost prestige. Three of the four West Indian reserves, Derek Parry, David Murray and Larry Gomes, had a rare chance of a match, and Murray and Parry both did well. The promising Malcolm Marshall, unfortunately, was unfit.

The remarkable feature of these last two qualifying games was the size of the crowd in both cases. In Adelaide just under 25,000 people went to see a match not involving Australia, and in Sydney 17,000 went along on a stifling evening to cheer on the home team even though they could no longer qualify. The reason for the attraction of the Adelaide match was partly the magnetic quality of the West Indian cricketers – Viv Richards in particular – and partly the fact that this was the only major international match of the season in Adelaide, apart from the

Test match. Nevertheless, the fact that this was a bigger crowd than any attracted to Sydney for any match all season demonstrated the pulling-power of one-day cricket itself. The crowds for matches of longer duration played by both West Indies and England in Adelaide earlier in the season had attracted miserable attendances. This, however, was partly because PBL, the promoters, had put all their eggs into the limited-over basket. The constant publicity which they gave to the one-day internationals (and earlier in the year to the domestic one-day tournament, the McDonald's Cup) certainly paid off, whereas the policy (if such it was) of ignoring any other matches apart from the Tests contributed towards the small crowds attending those.

The Finals

Kerry Packer's assertion that people will pay to watch the best seemed to be justified by the crowd of 30,196 who came to Melbourne on an ideal summer's day on 20 January to see the first of the 'best of three' finals. Brearley won the toss, a good one to win with the game starting at ten o'clock and some early moisture in the pitch.

The West Indies decided on the extra bowler rather than the extra batsman, restoring Colin Croft in place of Lawrence Rowe, who had proved superfluous because of the way in which Richards, Greenidge and Kallicharran had dominated the scoring in the earlier games. England's team contained two changes from the combination which had done most of the work to get them into the finals. Derek Underwood was left out in favour of John Emburey, a realistic decision, and Wayne Larkins was preferred to Derek Randall. The vital question about England's team, however, had been whether or not Geoff Boycott would rule himself fit after missing the previous two games because of the bruised finger joint suffered during the Sydney Test a fortnight before. Much to his colleagues' relief, Boycott said after practice at the MCG on the day before the match that although he did not consider himself to be one hundred percent fit he would play if the selectors wished him to. They did, of course. Boycott was, apart from

Gooch, the only batsman to have achieved any sort of consistency; indeed he had seldom played better in his life. An X-ray had shown no damage to his finger – bruised when it was struck by a ball from Len Pascoe during the Sydney Test – and a specialist had been unable to find anything wrong. Other members of the England team had bruises, and Viv Richards, like Boycott the key member of his side, had set a selfless example by playing in every match for the West Indies despite his hip and groin injuries which ought, in his own long-term interests, to have been rested. Instead Richards often played with the aid of a pain-killing injection.

In short, Boycott had a duty to play. Yet on the eve of the match he created for himself yet another of those incidents which had caused him to lose the captaincy of both his county and his country. During a long telephone conversation with a kite-flying journalist, Boycott unwisely aired grievances which apparently stemmed from his umbrage at being left out of the first limited-over game of the season. At the time, on the evidence of Boycott's form over the previous year both in England and Australia, that decision had been logical. Boycott had quickly proved it wrong, however, by playing so well that he again became the most important batsman in the side. Then the gremlin in the Boycott soul which seemed to command 'self-destruct' whenever he apparently had the world at his feet became active again. As I have related earlier in the book, he had a minor contretemps with Brearley before the first Test, then was unwilling to play in the second because of his stiff neck. He then missed two limited-over internationals because of his bruised finger.

Of course one had sympathy that he should be obliged to play under any sort of handicap, but it was impossible to agree with the wild claims he was reported to have made after his telephone conversation. The reporter quoted Boycott as saying that he was 'fed up with the whole set-up' on the tour, that he had told the selectors that he was not fit but they would not listen, and that they were 'taking it out on me because no one else can get any runs.' It was the old persecution complex rearing its head again. Boycott said he believed that he was speaking off the record to the reporter, who worked for ITN news but also filed a report to the *Sunday Telegraph*. The reporter claimed that he had not been instructed that the remarks were not to be quoted and he was unaware of the unwritten etiquette of a cricket tour which demands that any controversy likely to disturb the team's morale should be referred first to the manager before it is publicised.

When this classic storm in a teacup broke in Australia, England had already played the first final with the West Indies and Boycott had played his part in what turned out to be a thrilling game.

Willis and Botham began the match with some testing opening overs, and Greenidge and Haynes were unable to make their normal free start. Both, in fact, survived confident early l.b.w. appeals by Willis, who had figures of one for 12 in an excellent six-over spell. Haynes was his victim, caught off the inside edge by the admirable Bairstow in the seventh over.

It was Dilley, however, after Greenidge had collected seven runs off his first two balls, who took the vital wicket of Richards. After hitting two streaky fours to fine third-man he got an under-edge to a cut. But the substance of the West Indies innings was provided by Greenidge and Kallicharran who added 95 in 20 overs. Willey was the most punished bowler during the stand, yet he should have had Kallicharran caught at deep square-leg by Boycott for 26. It looked very much as though a momentary subconscious flinching by Boycott, obviously because the injured finger was on his mind, caused the error, but his batting later more than made up for the lapse. Two other missed chances, however, were to prove crucial in the final analysis. Greenidge had been missed off a hard return chance to Botham when he was only six. He went on to bat magnificently in making 80, by far the biggest score of the day. Then, with the West Indies losing wickets fast in various ways, the last serious danger to England, Collis King, was missed by Gower at mid-wicket when he was only five. He appeared to be lucky to be given not out when Gooch hit the stumps with a fine throw soon after and stayed to plunder 31 vital runs, including a monumental six off Willis. The West Indies scored 34 runs off the last four overs. When the match reached its climax, England needed to score 34 off *five* overs.

England's innings made fascinating watching because their target of 216 was never out of reach. Yet the West Indies, fielding superbly, managed to take wickets just often enough to keep the pressure on their opponents. Gooch fell to a brilliant catch at mid-wicket off a cleanly struck pick-up shot; Boycott, having batted with skill and confidence, was caught off a similar shot for 35, another fine catch; and Gower went through with a drive against a slower ball from the wily Roberts.

Between the 28th and 39th overs the Northamptonshire pair of Willey and Larkins guided England into a position from which victory ought to have been gained with relative comfort. Willey gradually worked out how to counteract the awkward high bounce of Garner and the consistent legside attack by Croft, and Larkins, who had earlier taken a fine catch in the deep, batted with a composure and tactical sense which suggested a happy future. Cutting, gliding and stroking with quiet skill he made 34 from 42 balls, helped by Lloyd's extensively deep field-setting. Then, at 152, Willey went in search of a second run and was brilliantly thrown out by Alvin Kallicharran. (I felt special sympathy for Willey because once, in a county second eleven match a long time before, I had taken a similar chance with the little man's speed and throwing power and suffered the same fate.)

The run-out of Wayne Larkins which followed soon after was more unfortunate and unusual. Larkins drove a ball hard back at the bowler, Garner, who deflected the ball onto the stumps at the bowler's end with the non-striker, Botham, just getting back in time. The ball deflected off the stumps to Haynes at mid-on who quickly picked up and scored a direct hit on the other set of stumps whilst Larkins was looking vaguely for an impossible run.

England were now 164 for five, in the 42nd over. Botham and the new batsman, Brearley, did their best to keep the momentum going but by now Roberts and Holding were the bowlers with overs to spare, and the going was not easy, with Lloyd setting ultra-defensive fields.

28 runs were needed from the last four overs. In the 47th over Botham was the victim of another marvellous catch, this time by Lloyd, and 25 runs were needed off the last three overs. Running as if the flames of hell were at their heels, Brearley and Bairstow reduced the target to 19 off two overs, 15 off the last. The palms began to sweat and the lips to go dry as Bairstow struck two to long-on off the first ball, Murray let a bye from the second and Brearley swung the third heroically to

square-leg for a precious boundary. Eight runs were needed from the last three balls: Brearley on-drove the fourth and, helped by an overthrow, the batsmen ran a desperate three. Five needed off two balls! Bairstow swung furiously but mistimed and scored only a single to deep mid-on. Brearley, needing only three from the last ball (because England had lost fewer wickets and would have won a tied game), managed to hit Holding's full-length delivery to the legside but not quite hard enough, and Bairstow was run out going for an impossible second run. England had lost by two runs.

The West Indian victory in the second of the finals was much more commanding and much less exciting. A Sydney crowd of 20,840, a little above the average attendance for all the one-day internationals, saw the reigning world limited-over champions coast to an eight-wicket win with three overs and four balls to spare. Despite ideal batting conditions England were unable to score a total big enough to put substantial pressure on the West Indies batsmen, and again Gordon Greenidge and Viv Richards rose nobly to the occasion.

Brearley once more won the toss and Boycott and Gooch gave England's innings the necessary solid start, putting on 40 before Gooch was l.b.w. to Garner hitting across the line. Although Boycott played superbly, moving his feet into position with remarkable speed so that he was always in position to hit the ball where he wanted to, only Gower and Botham of the others found much of an answer to some more ruthlessly efficient West Indian bowling. Brilliant instinctive cricketers Lloyd's men may be, but the captain planned his one-day tactics with care and his team carried them out with admirable discipline.

The only weakness, indeed, in the West Indies side as a limited-over force was the lack of a fifth bowler who was anything more than adequate. Gower and Boycott managed to take most of the 57 runs which came off ten overs from Richards and King, but the return of Holding removed Gower to an exclusively 'one-day' shot (trying to tickle a ball through the slips), and when Boycott was caught on the very edge of the square-leg boundary accepting Roberts's invitation to hook, the innings went into decline. Botham, it is true, hit three fours and a crashing six into the pavilion off Roberts, and Bairstow hustled 18 runs at the end, but the run-rate of just

Gordon Greenidge at last showed Australian crowds the brilliant batting familiar
to spectators in Hampshire and Barbados. In the One-Day Internationals he was
England's major scourge, top-scoring in both the finals. Leg-theory could not
reduce his range of stroke during his 80 in Melbourne. *Above* Willey is swept;
below Bairstow watches a crunching square-cut.

England's successes. *Above left* Gooch worked hard on his technique and had a much more successful tour than his first to Australia the year before. *Above right* Brearley had a better tour with the bat, although his captaincy lost its magic touch. *Below* Boycott took coloured pads and the one-day games in his stride. At times his batting was almost carefree.

The new order and the old. *Above* Channel 9 commentator David Colley (ex-Australia) gets an instant opinion of the controversial pitch at the start of the Sydney Test. *Centre* The crowd at Melbourne has another go at the England captain. *Below* Sir Donald Bradman talks to Clive Lloyd during the Adelaide Test.

Above Thomson bowls during his disastrous second spell in the last of the One-Day Internationals against England. Emburey is the batsman, Bairstow the non-striker. *Below* Lillee's arm is still high; he went from strength to strength, but Thomson was soon discarded.

above four an over on a blameless, bland Sydney pitch did not ask enough of the West Indies.

Nevertheless, England had given themselves a sporting chance, and another tense match seemed possible. It was not to be because Greenidge and Haynes set off with a succession of brilliant shots. Greenidge in particular was charged up and tuned to perfection. For some reason Brearley changed his policy of giving Botham the new ball, but if he had hoped for a dominating burst by Willis and Dilley he was quickly disappointed. The West Indies batsmen made them look like medium-pacers and when Botham came on to dismiss Haynes l.b.w. as he essayed one of the wild swings which at present mar his talented batting, Richards soon took smooth control.

Just for a time the duel between Richards and Botham, close friends and true sporting titans, was absorbing. Richards cover-drove him for four but was then rapped over the pads and survived an optimistic appeal before Botham, digging a ball in short, twisted a knee and had to limp off the field. He returned later none the worse but when Dilley came on in his place Richards hooked and drove him for fours at once and never faltered thereafter. He was eventually caught by Botham off a skier from Willey, an appropriate dismissal because Botham and Willey were England's outstanding bowlers in an unequal struggle. The admirable Greenidge just missed a century – indeed disdained to hit a deliberate full-toss from Gooch which might have given him the necessary six – but with a full half an hour of permissible floodlit time remaining the West Indies won the Cup, the £16,000 first prize and a £1,000 bonus for Greenidge as 'man of the series'.

The third of the scheduled finals was sensibly cancelled. As Michael Melford drily observed in the *Daily Telegraph*, this was the spoonful of sugar which made the medicine of an England defeat go down. Whatever the Sydney public may have wanted, the journalists had been glutted with one-day internationals. Instead of spending my final night at Sydney watching cricket I saw the Australian Opera Company's lively performance of *Patience* by Gilbert and Sullivan in the spectacular setting of the opera house. In the interval a P & O liner, the *Sea Princess*, cruised past, its creamy hull a mass of tiny lights silhouetted against the long curve of the harbour bridge. The passengers gazed at the Opera House and the theatre-goers gazed back at the liner in mutual admiration as soft music played from the top deck of the ship. A few hours before, President Jimmy Carter had warned of world war in his State of the Union message, but it was difficult to be pessimistic at this moment. Earlier in the day I had been taken round the sun-drenched harbour by Diana Fisher of *Women's Weekly* and Peter Doyle, whose family has fished in Sydney harbour for five generations. It had been a perfect, breezy sunny day, and as we sailed over the sparkling blue water amongst boats ranging from tiny dinghies to a RAN battleship one could appreciate the pride with which Doyle asked: 'Who'd ever swap Heaven for this, mate?'

Chapter Nine

FIVE-DAY WONDERS TOO!

The quaint, old-fashioned business of Test cricket began anew on 26 January, Australia Day (commemorating the arrival of Captain Philip in 1788). The broader canvas of the five-day game and the tranquil beauty of Adelaide made a pleasing contrast to the clamorous frenzy of Sydney night cricket. Indeed, there is no finer setting for Test cricket than the Adelaide Oval, unless, perhaps, it is Newlands at Cape Town where the handsome Table Mountain looms so close. A work-study had already been completed into the possibility of installing floodlights at Adelaide, and the most expensive scheme involved retractable towers which could be raised or lowered like telescopes to decrease their effect on the rest of the environment when the lights were not in use. But it would be a terrible shame to scar a beautiful ground just for the benefit of a television company. One of the most interesting statistics of the season, as I shall discuss later, is that, for all the attraction of night cricket, the average crowd for the eight night games at Sydney was only 15,800. For the Sydney Test, despite a rain-ruined first day, the average daily crowd was 18,626, and for the daytime one-day internationals held outside Sydney – three at Melbourne and one each at Adelaide and Brisbane – the average attendance was 26,014.

The only light in evidence when the Test began shone brightly from a cloudless sky. In a brief ceremony before the start of play the Australian flag was raised to the strains of 'Advance Australia Fair'. We returned to earth at once, however, with the inevitable 'Come on, Aussie, Come on' as Greg Chappell led his team onto the field having become only the second Australian captain ever to put the opposition in to bat in an Adelaide Test. Graham Yallop had been the first, twelve months before, his decision then being justified by a very green pitch, although not by the eventual result. Chappell had less justification, for the pitch looked a beauty. Nor was he to find much solace in the four-and-a-bit days' cricket which followed. Except for a superbly contested first day it was destined to be a very one-sided match.

That first day, however, was something to be savoured. Lillee, running in at full bore from the River Torrens end, struck the first blow for Australia when he had Greenidge l.b.w. with the last ball of his second over. But Viv Richards was soon showing Lillee, and everyone else, exactly who was boss. He began his breathtaking innings with an imperious off-drive off Lillee for four. Then he straight-drove Dymock for a second boundary, and when Pascoe replaced Lillee Richards made this fierce fast bowler look like a harmless tyro. He hooked Pascoe for a crunching four, then two balls later leg-glanced him to the same boundary with the finesse of a great artist.

Haynes settled in to a sensible, largely defensive innings at the other end whilst Richards, in an amazing spell of total domination, collected no fewer than six boundaries off nine balls delivered to him by Pascoe and Ashley Mallett.

Mallett had been recalled to Test cricket at the age of 34 in place of the leg-spinner Higgs. In the next two Tests, although only moderately successful, he was to show that his bowling had lost none of its accuracy or skilfully varied flight. Indeed he had earned his recall on merit after a successful season in the Sheffield Shield, to which he had returned after announcing his retirement in the earliest days of World Series Cricket. He had quickly become disenchanted with WSC after being hit on the head by a bouncer.

For a few overs on his return to the highest level he must have wished that he had remained a full-time journalist, because Richards drove both him and Pascoe time and again to the offside boundary, usually past motionless fielders. It was a marvellous demonstration of his rare virtuosity, and it was not just the skill of his driving, cutting and pulling which amazed one but also the very conception of some of the shots he played and the fact that he was carrying out this wholesale attack on the first morning of a Test match. It was almost irreverent. By lunchtime he had scored 76 off 70 balls with 13 fours, and one feared for Australia if he got going again after the break. He did not do so, however, because Lillee persuaded him to try a rash cut with fatal results in the first over of the afternoon. This marked the start of a determined

Australian fightback in which the tanned and husky Lillee and the pale, lean Mallett played the most prominent roles. Mallett followed the dethroning of Richards by having Haynes caught at backward square-leg, miscuing a wild swing. Thus in the first two overs after lunch 115 for one became 115 for three.

Despite being hit so brilliantly through the covers by Richards at the start of his spell, Mallett persisted with his refreshing off-stump line (few *English* off-spinners have not nowadays become obsessed with the leg-stump as a result of too much limited-over cricket) and he once or twice had Kallicharran stretching to get to the pitch of well-flighted deliveries. It was to one such that Kalli, the last of the West Indies form-horses, moved out to drive but only got a tickle and edged to Ian Chappell via Marsh's gloves.

At 126 for four West Indies fortunes were left in the hands of two men who had been desperately short of match practice, Lawrence Rowe and Clive Lloyd. Though they scored at nothing like the giddy rate of the morning, these two got their heads down and gradually settled in. At tea West Indies were 166 for four, and after it Lloyd began another devastating assault on the Australian bowlers, driving almost every delivery with brutal power either on the up or on the half-volley. Mallett, who had been so economical and testing before tea, was driven out of the attack and Pascoe found the weight of Lloyd's blade almost as heavy as Richards's. As a variation on the drive Lloyd sometimes went right back on to his stumps when a bowler pitched short and cut savagely past point. It was the second spectacular innings of a memorable day's cricket watched by 26,569 people in that almost country-town atmosphere unique to Adelaide.

Rowe played a most valuable innings in support and was just starting to take control himself, with supple late cuts and flowing drives, when he became the first victim of the ever-reliable and persistent Dymock. There was no luck for Rowe in the way that he unerringly found the only deep legside fielder as he picked the ball deftly off his toes, but Lillee needed to move quickly at deep backward square-leg to take the catch.

Lillee, indeed, was to have the final word, but not before Lloyd had surged on to his 12th Test century and his first for three years since one against Pakistan at Bridgetown shortly before the Packer revolution. This was the crowning moment for Lloyd in a tour which had begun disastrously for him and his team but which was now ending so well. Just before the close, however, he was out to Lillee who, in the last over of the day, had taken the new ball. Lloyd had been beaten by the previous delivery and he shaped to play to leg to the next ball and was obviously disappointed when umpire O'Connell, never afraid to give an l.b.w. decision (as so many Australian umpires are), upheld Lillee's trenchant appeal. To complete a tigerish performance Lillee bowled Roberts with the last ball of the day and, at 303 for 8, the honours of a day of splendid cut-and-thrust were clearly shared.

The second day was altogether less exciting, partly because it was a good deal more one-sided and partly because it was occupied mainly by the four West Indian fast bowlers pounding away remorselessly at the Australian city wall. By the end of the day it had crumbled and the invaders were safely inside, the Sir Frank Worrell Trophy all but won.

The West Indies made another 25 runs for their last two wickets which fell to Lillee and Pascoe. Garner was out to a particularly good slip catch by Hughes, whose cricket seemed to get better with every match. Lillee, playing in only his 37th Test, had taken five wickets in a Test innings for the thirteenth time.

The counter-assault by the West Indies fast bowlers opened with some hostile but wayward overs from Roberts and Holding. Laird looked much the more comfortable of the two Australian openers but there was not much that either of them was forced to play at first. Gradually, however, the two destroyers moved closer to the target and when they broke through they did so with a vengeance. Holding began by having Wiener well caught at close short leg by Haynes and in the next over Roberts swept away the Chappell brothers who had between them scored ten hundreds against the West Indies in the past. Ian pushed tentatively and was well taken at second slip; Greg, first ball, received a leaping delivery which carried off the shoulder of the bat into the gully. Roberts was engulfed by delighted colleagues whilst Australia's captain walked back through a stunned silence.

That they went on to reach 200 after thus being reduced to 26 for three spoke well of the Australians' determination, but they were forever like Sisyphus pushing a boulder uphill. Hughes and Laird looked the most likely to get to the top, adding 57 for the fourth wicket by brave and disciplined batting. Hughes three times hit Garner backward of point off the back foot but there was seldom much given away by any of the West Indies fast bowlers. It was the least vaunted of them, Croft, who turned in the day's outstanding performance, at one point bowling fourteen overs unchanged from the cathedral end under a very hot sun. He had Hughes caught at first slip by angling the ball across the right-hander from round the wicket and then finally rid the West Indies of the stubborn Laird, who sliced a drive into the all-enveloping hands of Garner in the gully. Laird had batted for three hours in making his fourth fifty in five innings against the West Indies fast bowlers. His runs had come from neat drives and glances and he had once again proved that courage and a sound technique are worth more in Test cricket than an abundance of natural talent.

Coming in at number six, Border, fresh from the double hundred he had made for New South Wales against Queensland the previous weekend, played solidly from the start. His form showed the advantages to Australia in the programme which had in other respects been unfavourable to them, because whereas touring batsmen who lost form had little chance to re-find it, Australians left out of the one-day side could get down to some solid match practice over four days in the Sheffield Shield.

Border must have been relieved to be going in three places lower in the order than he had been accustomed to, but he now suffered the disadvantage of being left with only tailend batsmen for support. Marsh would once upon a time have been considered a more than useful number seven at Test level but he had lost the secret during two years with WSC and he soon succumbed again, pushing forward and edging Croft to the wicket-keeper.

132 for six at tea, the Australians took longer to go down than the West Indies must have hoped. Border picked up runs with some neatly timed strokes whilst Lillee, despite being struck painfully on the right hand by a ball from Holding, battled bravely for just under an hour and Dymock for more than forty minutes. Mallett fell to a particularly brilliant slip

catch and Australia ended the day at 201 for nine, Border 54 not out. They had no real cause to reproach themselves, for the West Indian fast bowlers, even on as good a pitch as this one, were simply too good for most contemporary sides, especially when, as on this occasion, all the close catches were unerringly taken.

Roberts took the last wicket in the second over of the third day, a national holiday in celebration of Australia Day. But there was little for patriots to celebrate as the West Indies tightened their stranglehold in hot weather. West Indian teams of other eras might have thrown the bat with a lead of 125 to build on, but not this side of hardened professionals, who went about the business of making themselves unbeatable by calculated batting on a near-perfect pitch. Haynes and Greenidge laid the foundations efficiently, Haynes playing excellently until Pascoe had him caught behind off a ball which got just enough movement to take the outside edge.

Pascoe greeted Richards with a fiery burst of three bouncers in four balls. Two of them were no-balls and, in any case, it was sound and fury signifying nothing to Richards. He proceeded serenely to eight not out at lunch and then played strokes all round the wicket during the afternoon session. He started with successive driven fours off Lillee, one through extra-cover, the second past mid-on. During the course of Lillee's next three overs he scored boundaries from a cut backward of point and a hook to square-leg. When he turned his attention to Mallett he began with a straight-driven four for *hors d'oeuvres,* chose a well-roasted square-cut as his main course and finished with a sweep. Richards's 50 came in eighty minutes off sixty balls and included eleven fours. Greenidge, once again playing thoroughly well in support, had four fours in his 50, reached some twenty minutes later and with no real attempt to hurry the hundred partnership arrived at in better than even time. It was the happiest surprise for Australia when Border, given an exploratory over by Chappell before tea, bowled Richards off the inside edge as he shaped to crash the ball through the covers off the back foot. The lead at tea was 309.

Greenidge was 63 not out at the interval and so solidly was he playing that his first Test hundred against Australia appeared certain. But at 213 he moved down the pitch to drive

Mallett, misjudged the flight and found himself yorked, the ball squeezing under the bat to Marsh who took the bails off smartly to make belated amends for muffing a hard chance off Dymock when Greenidge was only nine. Greenidge's success on this tour was a delight to those who had seen him develop into a world-class player in England.

Kallicharran and Rowe, playing with such fluency and confidence that the two balls after Greenidge's dismissal were both hit for four, quickly built further on the massive West Indian lead. On a heavenly evening, with the mellow brown stone of St Peter's cathedral and the dark green of the Morton Bay fig trees etched clear against the cloudless blue sky, it was pleasing cricket for the objective viewer, but though Australia bowled tightly and fielded better than at any time all season (Hughes was outstanding in the deep) at least half of the 17,636 members of the crowd went home early, tired of the one-way traffic. Those who did missed Rowe being caught behind cutting at Dymock after a stand of 86 in 71 minutes with Kallicharran, but Croft held out successfully for ten minutes as nightwatchman.

The West Indies lead at the start of the fourth day was 428 and Chappell took the new ball as soon as it became due after one over. But it was not until the thirteenth over of the day that Croft was removed. The ball was keeping low at times but the pace of the pitch was slower and neither Kallicharran nor Lloyd looked anything less than comfortable. Lloyd was, however, dropped by Greg Chappell at slip, slicing an intended force off the back foot off Dymock when he had scored only four. It was the signal for Kallicharran to tuck into Pascoe at the other end, off-driving and then hooking for successive fours in an over which cost 14 runs and saw the total past 350. Pascoe was learning in this match the hard lesson that against good batsmen on good wickets speed without accuracy is ineffective.

Kallicharran reached his 12th Test hundred in his 54th Test with a drive and a cut off Mallett. He celebrated with a thunderous hook off Lillee before chopping an intended cut off Mallett and departing to a generous reception at the end of another brilliant innings during the course of which he had become the sixth West Indian (after Weekes, Sobers, Kanhai, Lloyd and Fredericks) to reach 4,000 Test runs. It is interesting that four of the six most prolific batsmen from the

Caribbean should have been left-handed. Kallicharran has always been a marvellous strokeplayer, neat, technically straight and sound, with a crisp, precise timing and admirable ability to play the kind of innings best suited to any situation.

At lunch the West Indies lead was 534 but Lloyd, no doubt mindful that India had scored 445 in the fourth innings at Adelaide two years before, batted on for a further 45 minutes into the afternoon session, Australia finally having to bowl the West Indies out to get another chance to bat. The captain himself was caught behind off the admirable 'Dimmick', as the Australians usually call him, almost straight after lunch, and the subsequent efforts of the tailenders seemed pointless. It was a case of Aussie-bashing, with the indignities heaped onto Lloyd's side by Greg Chappell, Dennis Lillee and others in 1975/76 no doubt still fresh in the memory of those who suffered them. Dymock was not complaining, however. He took the last three wickets on top of Lloyd's to finish with five in an innings for the fifth time in his seventeen Tests.

It was one of the few things Australians had to cheer about, for the home team went under in their second innings with scarcely a fight. Luck was against them, as it is against most teams in this sort of hopeless position. Their target of 574 in 542 minutes was quite clearly an impossible one. True to the formula of the first innings, Laird and Border proved the most difficult of the frontline batsmen to dislodge. Laird batted for an hour and 40 minutes but seemed very lucky to be given not out caught behind early in his innings when cutting at Holding. In the end Laird was l.b.w. and looked less than happy with the decision given against him by the same umpire, Max O'Connell. Ian Chappell may also have been unfortunate when hooking at Holding and being given out caught behind, because the ball may have struck his helmet rather than his bat. At all events he was hooking too early for safety. Indeed there seemed altogether a reluctance by Australia to buckle down and fight. Greg Chappell hit Croft for five fours but was then l.b.w., and Hughes had a most uncomfortable stay before he went in the same way. Border's plucky effort lasted 70 minutes but he was out cutting and it seemed that the West Indian fast bowlers simply had to attack Border around the off-stump and, sooner or later, he would succumb. For England's bowlers the policy did not work so well!

131 for seven on the fourth evening, Australia lost their last three wickets to the human gazelle, Michael Holding, on the fifth morning. At twenty to twelve the West Indies recorded a victory by 408 runs. Only five teams in the history of Test cricket have won a match by a bigger runs margin, and this was Australia's heaviest defeat since England beat them by 675 runs in 1928-29, Don Bradman's first Test, at the Exhibition ground in Brisbane.

For the West Indies it was extremely sweet revenge after the five-one defeat by Australia four years before, and this was the first rubber they had ever won in six tours of Australia. They set off the very next day for a tour of New Zealand and were promptly defeated, in very different conditions, in the first Test in Dunedin where New Zealand triumphed by a single wicket. Upsets will happen but, barring a prolonged continuation of the injury to Viv Richards, there seemed no reason why Lloyd's side should not remain generally too good for all opponents. Richards was allowed to miss the trip to New Zealand, where he was badly missed, so that he could rest the injury which had plagued him all season. It stemmed from a hairline fracture at the base of his spine, but despite it this greatest of contemporary batsmen had made 1077 runs in only 14 innings during the tour. In the Tests he made 386 runs at an average of 96.5 and in the one-day internationals 545 runs at 109. It merely confirmed what one had long suspected: that Viv Richards is the best batsman since Bradman.

The new maturity of Richards was one reason why much the same West Indies side had been beaten five-one by Greg Chappell's Australians only four years before but had now emerged triumphant. The previous West Indies side had been at least as strong on paper; indeed essentially it was the same. Lloyd had been captain, Roberts and Holding the opening bowlers, with Boyce and Holder (two fine cricketers) in support instead of Croft and Garner. The presence of the great off-spinner Lance Gibbs had given the 1975-76 side greater variety and the batting had been stronger on paper, with Fredericks added to Richards, Lloyd, Kallicharran, Greenidge and Rowe. The side, in fact, had improved greatly during the 1976 tour of England when the combination of four fast bowlers was tried successfully for the first time, with Holder and Wayne Daniel in the place of Garner and Croft. Sadly for the game as a spectacle the strategy of a continual pace bombardment had proved highly effective. It was awe-inspiring to realise that in Daniel, Malcolm Marshall, Sylvester Clarke and Norbert Philip the West Indies had four reserve fast bowlers who would all be knocking at the door of most other contemporary Test sides.

Lloyd and his shrewd deputy Deryck Murray deserved much of the credit for their team's success, both in planning the campaign so well and in ensuring that the team quickly bounced back from any reverses (notably from their bad start to the tour) by remaining mentally and physically fit. Lloyd himself believed that the greatest reason of all for the fact that a West Indian side had for the first time done full justice to its abilities in Australia was the fact that his men had toured Australia three years running (twice with WSC) and had at last come to terms with hard grounds, bigger arenas, a hostile atmosphere (unlike in England, where there is so much Caribbean support) and opponents who give no quarter. In success he was able to make criticisms both of the standard of Australian umpiring and of the 'antics' and abusive language of the Australian players. As far as the antics were concerned his own side were definitely not exempt from criticism and nor were England.

The final question of the long Australian summer was now about to be answered. Could England follow up the West Indies victory and prove their captain's assertion that they were as good a side as Australia? Certainly, after such a defeat and with only one day intervening between the fifth and sixth Tests, the opportunity was open.

Chapter Ten

ENGLAND BLOW IT

The story of the unsatisfactory mini-series between Australia and England in 1979-80 was, from an English point of view, one of chances missed. The Melbourne Test was no exception.

At Perth England could say at the end: 'If only we had not thrown it away by bad batting on the final day!'; at Sydney: 'If only we had not lost the toss!' Now, at Melbourne, having won the toss and gained first use of the most placid pitch imaginable, they could say when their first innings closed shortly before two o'clock on the second day: 'If only we had made the most of an ideal start!'

One man in particular had cause to think deeply about what might have been, the softly-spoken Essex opener Graham Gooch. With Geoff Boycott he laid the foundation of a huge total, then proceeded to the very edge of the greatest moment of his life, only to throw it all away in the most decisive moment of the entire game.

Australia made only one change to their Adelaide eleven, McCosker returning in place of Wiener. England's side showed two changes from the eleven defeated at Sydney; Wayne Larkins, fresh from a fine innings of 90 in the three-day match against New South Wales at Canberra, replaced Derek Randall, who had grafted for 44 when England were in trouble at Canberra but been unable to go on to a big score, and John Lever came back for Graham Dilley, who was suffering from a strained side. Lever might have returned in any case and Bob Willis, who had laboured in vain to find any of his old spark, was fortunate to play, especially as Stevenson had taken the first four New South Wales wickets in Canberra. It was to be, in all probability, Willis's final Test match. Several others in the team – Mike Brearley, Bob Taylor, Geoff Boycott and Derek Underwood – must have walked across the paddock from their hotel to the Melbourne Cricket Ground on the first morning of the match with a twinge of nostalgia. For all five, and perhaps Lever as well, it was likely to be their last Test in Australia.

Boycott has never scored a hundred at Melbourne, but at lunchtime on that first day he was well placed to do so. Play began with an uncharacteristically poor over from Lillee whose opening spell generally was indifferent and sharply in contrast to his form later in the innings. Indeed he left the field for the hour before lunch due to an 'indisposition', the nature of which was never made clear. Gooch and Boycott certainly took full advantage, starting with such comfort and positiveness that one could hardly believe this was an England opening pair. With Gooch driving imperiously and Boycott tucking the ball away into the gaps with solid assurance, 30 runs came from the first nine overs, and Mallett came on with his off-spinners to bowl only the tenth over of the match. But the pitch had as little in it for him as for anyone else, and Gooch soon showed his confidence by lofting Mallett for a handsome four over the bowler's head, then playing a lovely off-drive in the next, the ball scudding across the lush outfield for four.

Mallett's first four overs cost 28 runs, but in the course of them he ought to have had Boycott, then 15, caught by Ian Chappell at slip. Later Gooch, who has an unfortunate knack of getting himself out in mid-innings, as it were, perhaps because his subconscious tells him that having got to 30 or 40 he has not failed, tried to hit Mallett in the direction of mid-on, only to spoon the ball towards Dymock who, dashing in from long-off, could not hold on to a swirling skier.

Gooch reached 50 with a handsome square-cut off Mallett and at lunch England were 94 for no wicket, Boycott 37, Gooch 54. In the interval a trophy in memory of Sir Robert Menzies was presented to the Australian Cricket Board chairman Bob Parish by the acting Prime Minister Doug Anthony, whose superior Malcolm Fraser was in Washington discussing with President Carter the 'free world' response to the Soviet invasion of Afghanistan. The trophy will be played for on future England tours of Australia in a match against the Prime Minister's eleven at Canberra. After this presentation another was made to Alan McGilvray, my respected colleague in many a commentary-box, who was said to be broadcasting on an Anglo-Australian Test for the 100th time.

It was a hot and sultry day. The crowd, very small at first because of a power strike which had prevented some people from travelling by rail or tram, reached a mere 15,116 by the end of the day. At lunchtime the knowledgeable amongst them would probably have guessed at an England total by six o'clock of perhaps 270 for four. Optimistic Britons would have hoped for 300 for two. After all, the pitch was, in Graham Gooch's words, 'slow and flat', and a firm base had been laid. Lillee was reported to be 'crook' and the Australians looked tired after their demoralising defeat at Adelaide. But Australians are never so dangerous as when they are down, and this England side had shown in recent years a rare imagination when it came to working out ways to collapse.

Whilst the vastly experienced Boycott was at the crease there was always likely to be a sense of order and calm about the batting. But after he and Gooch had recorded the first century opening partnership by an England pair for three Test series (the same pair had added 111 against New Zealand at Trent Bridge in 1978), Boycott drove at Dymock and edged hard and low to the gully where Mallett, who had pulled off so many amazing catches in that position five years previously, dived to take a brilliant one-handed catch.

From 116 for one England advanced to 170 in a steady second-wicket partnership between Gooch and Larkins, who could hardly have hoped for better circumstances in which to launch his Test career than on a slow pitch and after such a good start. He had hit 25, stroking the ball with the full face of the bat in a manner which reminded Lindsay Hassett of Arthur Morris, when he sparred outside the off-stump against Pascoe and was caught at first slip.

The crucial moment of the whole game soon followed. Gooch, having hit ten fours, was approaching a maiden Test hundred. Mallett came off after bowling 25 overs unchanged from the southern end and Pascoe was joined in the attack by Lillee, now restored to health and permitted to bowl after an hour's fielding. He brought the sleepy crowd to life at last, getting the ball, somehow, to cut both ways off the seam. He beat Gooch more than once. The big man did not need to hurry but a hundred in a Test at Melbourne beckoned him on. He played a ball from Pascoe straight back down the pitch, just missing the stumps at the other end. Pascoe could not stop the ball on his follow-through and Gooch called his partner Gower to run. Hughes, running round from mid-off, picked up the ball and threw, off-balance, but directly in line with the three stumps at the non-striker's end. Gooch was out by a foot, the third man in the three Tests to miss a hundred by one run.

It was a personal tragedy for Gooch and a disaster for his team, who had looked to him not just for a hundred but for a major innings. England's larder door was open and that fierce competitor Lillee was through the gap like a hungry rat. Gower played loosely and a little across a ball that cut a fraction off the seam and was l.b.w. At the other end the hapless Willey, now more realistically placed at number five, repeated his horrific demise at Perth, padding up close to his off-stump and falling l.b.w. Then Botham, who in recent weeks had seemed to be batting better, flicked at a ball down the legside, and to his obvious dismay was given out caught behind. England had lost four wickets for seven runs and five for 22 since the fall of Larkins. In effect they had thrown the match away.

The Botham decision was declared on television evidence to be incorrect. If it was, one had every sympathy for the umpire, not just because it is desperately hard to tell whether a legside deflection has come off pad or bat (although the benefit of the doubt in such cases should be given to the batsman) but also because the verdict was given by a man of only 32 standing in his first Test match. The rise to Test status of Peter Cronin from Adelaide was remarkable in many ways, not least because he had previously stood in only four first-class matches and two one-day internationals. England had, like the West Indies before them although without making the matter public, objected to one of the umpires originally chosen for this Test, and Cronin had been the replacement on grounds of his good performances earlier in the season. There had, indeed, to be much official confidence in him for him to be given such high responsibility so young, and it was the more difficult for Cronin to win respect from the players because he himself had never played cricket at any level, except, he told me, for a few games at school. A personable fellow, he is immersed in cricket and although his lack of playing knowledge must be a disadvantage when it comes to making certain decisions or dealing with unusual situations, he talks a good deal to players and other umpires and says that he would give up his job with a finance company tomorrow if he were given the chance to become a full-time professional umpire. For this match he was paid £400 plus expenses. Australian umpiring has been inconsistent over the years and it might be a useful development to have professionals doing the job. As in every walk of life experience makes the job easier.

Botham's dismissal had reduced England to 192 for six. It had been a courageous fight-back by Australia, or another dismal middle-order failure by England, depending on how you looked at it. Certainly Lillee and Pascoe deserved much credit, but equally England had criminally wasted their ideal start. Fortunately for them two players brought up in the old school of county cricket, before the proliferation of limited-over games which seemed to have destroyed the understanding of the art of building an innings, now came together. Brearley and Taylor, by shrewd defence and playing straight on a benign pitch, lifted their team to 231 for six by the close of the hot afternoon.

An overnight thunderstorm seemed to have had some influence on the pitch when play began on Saturday before a crowd of 26,664, just large enough to make this seem more like a Melbourne Test. There had been times the previous day when, closing one's eyes, one might have guessed one was at Lord's on a Monday morning for the match between MCC and the touring team – except of course that Lord's would not have been so warm on a May morning. If there was any doubt that this was Australia – and the opponents the one enemy capable of really stirring the antipodean passions – it was soon removed when Brearley walked out to bat. He was booed from the 'outer' then; he was booed even louder when he walked in at the end of his innings undefeated with 60; and he was booed whenever he touched the ball (or tried unavailingly to touch it) later in the day. A Sunday paper devoted its front page the next day to a condemnation of the louts who jeered an England captain. Certainly he did not deserve such treatment, which had become fashionable and seemed to stem from his strong opposition at the start of the tour to many of the WSC innovations and then to his comments about unruly crowds making it dangerous sometimes for fielders to patrol the outfield. The fact was that his remarks had helped to stir the authorities to take sterner action against the small hooligan element in cricket crowds, resulting in much better behaviour in the second half of the season. I felt that there was no viciousness in the booing on this occasion. It was simply a new sport: Brearley-baiting. Brearley himself said that the only times he was disturbed by crowd hostility was when he felt he had no right to be on the field. On this tour he had played well enough to feel quite adequate in high company.

The captain's innings developed from an overnight 19 not out, first by solid defence and deft deflections, then by more fluent cover-drives and onside placements. He reached fifty with a delightful off-drive off Lillee which brought him his first boundary, and, on this occasion, the claps and cheers of the members provided a challenge to the boos from the south. Brearley raised his bat with justifiable pride. He had played a good innings which had saved his side from complete collapse.

Dennis Lillee was the other central character in the first part of the day. Using the moisture which made the pitch livelier for an hour or so he soon burst through Taylor's defences, the ball spinning back off a limp bat on to the stumps after a valuable innings of 88 minutes' duration. Underwood was the next to go, caught at second slip after a brief uncomfortable stay, but the admirable Lever batted with a straight bat and instinctive common sense for an hour and a half. He had contributed 22 to a ninth-wicket stand of 54 when, in the last over before lunch, Lillee conned him out by bringing up seven men around the bat. Lever, looking for a short ball, made a momentary flinching movement back and a straight good-length ball clean-bowled him. It was Lillee's 200th Test wicket in his 38th Test. With the aid of a lovely left-handed slip catch by Greg Chappell after lunch he took his figures to 6 for 60, the 14th occasion on which he has taken more than five wickets in a Test innings. At the age of 30 he joined only four other Australian bowlers who have taken more than 200 Test wickets: Benaud 248, McKenzie 246, Lindwall 228, and Grimmett 216.

Australia's innings began just after two o'clock. Lever and Botham took the new ball but McCosker picked up nine runs off Lever's second over and he was soon replaced at the southern end by Willis. The latter bowled very straight and to a good length, but these days, on a good wicket, this was not enough. His figures in his only really testing spell in the game were 7-3-10-0.

It was Underwood, coming on for the 20th over from the

northern end, who took the only Australian wicket to fall on the second day. McCosker had come close to being caught off Underwood at a short mid-on position at Sydney and when he had made a positive 33 he obligingly miscued a drive to Botham in that same position. But Laird, once more digging in and shaping his innings like a potter with clay, began, in company with Ian Chappell, the long process of putting the match out of England's reach. Once again England failed to take the half-chances. When 24 Laird edged a ball from Lever which bounced unexpectedly and hurried past Brearley at first slip – he lost sight of the ball in the crowd. When 13 Chappell drove too soon at Underwood but the bowler could not hold on to the return catch in his outstretched right hand. Neither batsman gave England a second chance and the scoring rate increased as the bowlers tired in the evening session. Both men reached excellent fifties before the close – in Laird's case his fifth in six Tests – and Australia finished the second day strongly placed at 155 for one.

There was a Sunday crowd of 39,102, the second biggest gate for any match in the whole season but poor by the standards of five years earlier. They saw Australia's strong position eroded in the morning session through some superb bowling by Underwood and some skilful England fielding, but then a mature innings by Border and a marvellously disciplined and graceful one by Greg Chappell made their side impregnable.

Ian Chappell had begun the day with a string of positive strokes, smearing the second ball of the morning for four over the slips off the luckless Willis. Devoid of all venom, however, England's main strike bowler was to be given only eight overs all day. The bulk of the work was done by Underwood, Lever and a Botham who at this stage of the tour was looking overweight and a little tired. Needless to say, he soon corrected that impression.

Laird was the first of Underwood's two morning victims, caught at mid-wicket off a rare full toss. Fifteen runs later Chappell, after playing some handsome drives, went through with another intended drive off Underwood, who had held the ball back skilfully and gleefully accepted the return catch. The two missed chances the previous day had cost England 112 runs. To complete a good morning for the visitors, however,

Brearley took the new ball at once and in the first over Hughes obligingly drove rather wildly at Botham and lofted the ball straight to mid-off. Another two wickets either side of lunch would have seen England back on level terms, for any slight lead by Australia would be cancelled out by their having to bat last on a pitch which was already taking a little spin and on which the ball was keeping increasingly low.

But Border and Greg Chappell, who had held himself back in the order because of soreness in the right knee and a sore throat, buckled down with admirable single-mindedness to take the initiative again. At lunch Australia were 224 for four. In the first hour afterwards they added only 38, restricted by tight bowling and good fielding, notably by Randall who came on as substitute for Larkins when the latter injured a finger as he tried to avoid a full-blooded hit by Border at short-leg. But Chappell and Border were well set by tea, the left-hander having reached fifty first with a square-cut off Lever and a crashing pull off Willey.

After the interval the fifth-wicket pair turned the screw, hitting from the attack-the one man who had really threatened them, the admirable Underwood. A little tired by now, he was struck for 13 in one over as Chappell, with cool brilliance, on-drove two fours, cut for one and then saw Border pulling a third boundary high over mid-wicket. Not long after this calculated assault, Chappell, who now had a tummy upset to add to his other ailments, retched by the side of the pitch. But he refused to give anything away, especially after Border had been caught-and-bowled by the deserving Lever, playing too early as he essayed an indeterminate shot off the back foot. He had played his full part in an outstanding and vital stand of 126, but he had been lucky in that Botham and Willis had persistently attacked his off-stump from round the wicket early in his innings instead of increasing the angle by going *over* the wicket like the West Indian bowlers. It was vital for Australia, who had to bat last, that Chappell should now sustain his effort and with great mental courage he did so, though he must have longed to relax. Although he scored 29 in the last hour, still driving with grace and placing the ball past mid-on off the back foot with a straight bat, he just failed to reach a hundred before stumps, much to the disappointment of a crowd roaring him on and booing the out-of-touch Marsh whenever the latter failed to give his partner the strike. Australia were 93 ahead at the close, 399 for five.

Chappell reached his hundred off the third ball of Tuesday morning, bringing up the 400. He was very nearly caught by a diving Botham off Lever's first delivery from the other end and celebrated his reprieve with a perfect on-driven four. But he played more false shots in the brief final phase of his innings than at any other time and Lever deserved his wicket.

Lever had begun by dismissing Marsh, caught at second slip cutting (a fine catch off the face of the bat by Botham) and he then took the most wanted wicket in the course of another unchanged spell from the southern end which, on this fourth morning, earned him figures of 13-4-22-3. The ball which got Chappell was one of the few Lever bowled that was not of perfect length, and the credit for the wicket belonged entirely to Larkins. It was a full toss, struck hard to mid-wicket where Larkins dived to his right and held a brilliant right-handed catch inches from the ground. Lever finished a good morning's work by having Lillee caught at mid-off, but Mallett and Dymock batted sensibly to boost the eventual Australian lead to 171. Botham dismissed both batsmen after lunch, Mallett being adjudged l.b.w. after playing some excellent shots.

England began batting at 2.15 and by teatime they had conjured up yet another crisis for themselves. Gooch was beaten by two balls in Lillee's first over, but settled in after that to play very well again, striking a majestic four off his toes off Lillee to mid-wicket and cover-driving Dymock with perfect timing for another in the first few overs.

At the other end, however, England were quickly at sixes and sevens. Boycott survived a confident appeal for a catch behind the wicket down the legside off Dymock, but a few balls later he lost his off-stump as, quite unaccountably, he failed to play a shot at an off-cutter delivered by Lillee from wide of the crease.

Confused by Greg Chappell's clever ploy of posting a silly mid-off and a silly mid-on, Larkins seemed no more likely to work out a coherent technique, failing to get his front foot properly forward on a pitch which, with the ball keeping so low, demanded a positive forward move. He was l.b.w. to Pascoe, shuffling across his crease. Then, most criminal of all, Gower was out in the last over before tea, hooking at a ball which pitched outside the off-stump and took the off-bail. It was not very short, and in any case hooking was a dangerous business against the short delivery because the ball was tending to keep so low.

In the evening Australia pressed home their advantage. Willey failed again when he was brilliantly caught low down the legside by Marsh off the thinnest edge. He had reached double figures only once in six Test innings in Australia.

Brearley came out at number six and for a time he and Gooch steadied the rapidly sinking ship. Lillee came off after another superb opening spell of 15 overs in which he had taken three wickets for 35. His leg-cutters, like fast leg-breaks, had made life very difficult for the batsmen, especially when they could not be certain that the ball was not going to cut back. A few years before he had tended on lifeless pitches to try to bowl flat out and dig the ball in. Now he bowled off a shorter run and managed to move the ball when others could not. Even the in-form Gooch was lucky to survive against him.

Mallett succeeded Lillee and, like Underwood before him, got a little spin from the pitch from the northern end. He it was who dismissed Gooch, who had hit six fours and made 51 out of 88 when he pushed forward, playing for spin which was not there, and was bowled.

Soon afterwards Brearley pushed forward to Pascoe and was unable to keep the ball down. Border at silly mid-off took the catch, once again justifying the special field-placing which Chappell had worked out for the increasingly awkward pitch. England were 92 for six.

From this nadir Ian Botham and Bob Taylor batted well and gradually batting was made to look a comfortable pastime again rather than an exercise in masochism. Botham belatedly reminded Australians what a superb striker of a ball he can be, notably when he hit a tiring Pascoe for successive fours, one a straight drive, the next an imperial force off the back foot. England ended the fourth day at 157 for six, still needing 14 to make Australia bat again.

It was one of those situations which can be retrieved only to a limited extent, but England managed to end the series on a high note, if not a winning one, thanks to some remarkable batting by Botham and a determined display of bowling and fielding which kept Australia waiting for their third victory until seven minutes into the last hour of the final day.

Botham at his best makes the game look wonderfully simple, and he adorned the final morning with a succession of cleanly struck, full-blooded blows uninhibitedly played from a high backlift and with a sweeping flow-through of the bat. More important, since we all knew that he could dominate any attack if he could only temper his natural ability with some discretion, he took care to place the ball carefully, to keep it along the ground most of the time, and to play the defensive stroke when one was demanded. Moreover he used delicacy of touch as well as his leonine strength, interspersing an array of handsome drives, mainly straight down the ground, with an occasional cut or a gentle legside dab. His maiden Test hundred against Australia deserved a full house but Botham could at least be sure that the 5,026 people scattered about the vast MCG stands were the genuine hard core of Australian cricket followers, able to appreciate to the full a brave innings in a cause that was almost certainly doomed.

Had Bob Taylor been able to get set again, of course, England's chances of saving the game were not necessarily gone. But he had added only four to his overnight score when he tried to hook – a most perilous stroke when the ball is keeping as low as it was – and merely skied a catch to silly mid-off. As in the first innings Underwood came and went quickly, this time softened up by Pascoe's previous ball, which hit him painfully on the hand, and then getting into line a little too late to the next delivery, but Lever again proved a tougher nut to crack. By cool defence, innate cricketing common sense and a very straight bat, he stayed with Botham until lunch, enabling England to set a target that was something more than a formality.

When he was 54 Botham hooked Lillee into, and out of, the hands of Dymock at deep square-leg, a scatter-brained shot because the trap had been plainly set. But this was the only blemish on a brilliant innings, and with a straight-driven four, his twelfth, he reached his fifth Test hundred in the last over before lunch.

Lillee calmed Australian fears soon after the break, in the fourth over with the second new ball, having Lever well caught off the glove after a courageous innings of an hour and three-quarters. Botham struck three more fours before Willis edged Pascoe low to Greg Chappell, who picked the ball up in one hand an inch from the ground and marched off like a man impatient to be home.

In the event Chappell *was* able to catch the last flight home to Brisbane only by his own brilliance, because it took Australia from a quarter-past two of a sunny afternoon until seven minutes past five of a cool evening to wrap up the series by three matches to nil. Botham, who had McCosker l.b.w. trying the fatal hook shot; Underwood, who eventually persuaded Laird to lose patience and sky a catch to mid-on; and Lever, who again bowled well and who thus crowned an excellent match which confirmed his ill-fortune in not being picked before, all chained the batsmen down, helped by some sparkling England fielding. But the elder Chappell dug in and refused to throw it away, before the younger one, unleashing a string of almost haughty strokes to show that even on a pitch now distinctly awkward he could make the game look easy, steered Australia home. There was something almost of Warwick Armstrong in the way that Greg Chappell waved on the 12th man shortly before the end and ordered him to put forward the time of the taxi which was to whisk him to the airport as soon as the game finished.

Greg Chappell and Dennis Lillee had made all the difference to an Australian side which, in other respects, was much of a muchness with the one beaten five-one by England the year before. Yet when one analyses England's failure, as opposed to Australia's success, it is apparent that the real decline was in the field rather than in the batting. After all, Rodney Hogg had taken 41 wickets in six Tests at 12 runs each in 1978-79 , as against Lillee's 23 in three Tests at 16 each, and England had scraped together more than 300 runs on only three occasions. This time improved form from Boycott and Gooch counteracted the even greater vulnerability of the middle order and the decline in particular of Gower and Randall.

In the field, however, England were altogether less sharp, missing some straightforward catches, accepting few of the half-chances which had been brilliantly snapped up the year before, and also failing to hit the stumps with throws which might have effected more of the unnerving and dispiriting run-outs which had plagued Australia under Yallop.

Brearley, who admitted that he might have taken a stricter line with some of his players, nevertheless claimed that

England had worked just as hard as the year before. One certainly observed no serious breaking of the team's spirit; indeed there were times when one felt that failures might have hurt the players more than they appeared to. It is cynical, perhaps, to point out that they were being paid very well whether they won or lost: to the 16 members of the touring party the difference between winning and losing each Test was just under £200 a man – the winning team earned £6,000 and the losing one £3,000. But it is clearly true that the more that players are paid as a basic fee, the less disastrous defeat becomes. On the other hand players knew that rivals would soon challenge their right to the big rewards now available to international cricketers if they did not produce successful performances.

More to the point, perhaps, is the fact that England's bowling, as well as their fielding, was significantly weaker. Willis had slipped over the brow of the hill and the promising Dilley is only at its foot as yet. Old's all-round qualities are not yet equalled by Stevenson. Miller's useful all-round work was missed. Above all, Hendrick was impossible to replace, and Lever, who would have come nearest to filling his shoes, was fatally omitted at Perth and Sydney before taking his rightful place at Melbourne and Bombay. Hendrick (whose close fielding was also badly missed) would have been well-suited by conditions in the first two Test matches and his remorseless accuracy would have hurried the Australian batsmen into more mistakes than they made. Moreover, his absence put extra responsibility on Botham, whose batting may have suffered as a result of his always being the bowler on whom Brearley looked as his chief shock, and stock, weapon.

As Australia were unfortunate to be thrashed five-one in 1978-79, so were England to be recorded as three-nil losers a year later. Small differences between two sides tend to be exaggerated in Test series, especially when one side makes the most of its opportunities and the other does not. But Australia proved themselves superior, their three Test victories being of much greater significance than their four defeats in the limited-over internationals. Test matches (I hope) will always remain the true test of a team's ability. England lost the final game at Melbourne, as they had the first at Perth, because they lacked certain qualities which are not essential to success in limited-over cricket, notably the ability to take wickets by attacking bowling and the art of building a long innings.

Ian Chappell, Border and Laird had shown how it could be done, but the supreme example was set by Greg Chappell, who had steeled himself to play the long innings necessary to shut the door on an England win. Lillee, named man of the match and of the series, was the other hero. A few years before he might have continued to bowl flat out on the slow Melbourne pitch, but by shortening his run and cutting his pace he had been able to cut the ball both ways in a demonstration of true artistry. Such is Lillee's will-power that had he come to England in 1977 I doubt if England would have won the Ashes in the Jubilee summer.

The chances were that Australia would put the record straight by taking the Ashes back after the series in England in 1981, although it must have worried the selectors that many of the mainstays of the team in this short and in many respects unsatisfactory series – Lillee, Marsh, Dymock and the Chappells – were nearer 40 than 20. But Laird, Border and Hughes were now established Test batsmen, Wiener was blooded, and bowlers like Lawson and Malone would soon get their chance.

England had fewer consoling thoughts as they packed their bags for India, the first leg of their journey home. Gooch had matured at last and Botham had put together a major Test innings against Australia. But Gower and Randall, the two 'flair' players, had much thinking to do about their techniques. Gower, no doubt, would be back on top of himself and the world before long. Such a (relative) failure was perhaps necessary to force him to appreciate that cricket demands even of its most brilliant exponents a good deal of thought and method.

The team would inevitably be changed during 1980. The loyal and admirable Willis had played perhaps two Test series too many but at least Dilley and Stevenson had been more or less blooded. Partly because of a lack of match practice Taylor's wicket-keeping was less consistent than normal, and Bairstow pushed him increasingly hard for the right to a Test place, although Taylor's exemplary performance in India at the end of the tour may have delayed the transition. Brearley had said that he would give up touring for a career as a psychotherapist – though he had no intention of retiring immediately – and Underwood and Boycott, though their outstanding quality had shone through the season, could not go on for ever. Of the younger batsmen Gower, Randall, Larkins and Willey would still be strongly in the running for Test places, but remained challenged by the likes of Parker, Cook, Gatting, Tavare and Williams.

Bob Woolmer and Phillippe Edmonds were also bound to come back into the reckoning. The two Northamptonshire batsmen, Peter Willey and Wayne Larkins, had mixed fortunes. Willey played some marvellous innings in the one-day games and he had no luck in the Tests in which his results were disastrous but hardly reflected his ability. Larkins seems to take a long time to settle in any company, and the movement of his feet seldom brought him positively forward or back. Yet his timing suggests a very good player who could still prove himself to be of Test class.

On the credit side, apart from Boycott's miraculous and admirable reincarnation, Graham Gooch worked hard on his technique and developed greatly. He should now be a cornerstone of England's batting for some time. He, and all the team, were well served by the management pair of Alec Bedser and Ken Barrington, both of whom worked willingly and effectively on a very demanding tour. As for the captain, the disappointment of defeat was tempered by the improvement in his own batting form. His Test average of 34 in this series more nearly reflects his ability than his previous Test career average of only 22. The truth lies somewhere in between, perhaps, but Brearley's contribution to cricket cannot begin to be evaluated by his batting average.

Consistency, not talent, is the missing quality among the batsmen of both England and Australia, but because of the hectic nature of first-class cricket at the start of the 1980s, the emphasis on limited-over cricket and on bonus points in county championship and Sheffield Shield, the general deterioration of pitches, and the more sustained and scientific use of fast and seam bowlers, one begins to doubt if either country will produce a batsman who, beginning his first-class career in 1980, is capable of scoring a hundred first-class centuries by the year 2000.

There is an additional reason why it is unlikely to happen. If the pace of the 1979-80 programme in Australia is to be the pattern for the future, no career is likely to last 20 years.

Chapter Eleven
CRICKET OVERKILL

This was to have been 'the most exciting season of cricket ever'. It turned out to be neither a sensational success nor a crashing failure. It was, of course, an experimental season. But if it satisfied the Australian Cricket Board and PBL, whose spokesmen produced some remarkably complacent statements at the end of the season, it pleased few of those who could stand back objectively and view the hectic season with the long-term interests of the game in mind. There was, as the foregoing pages testify, much outstanding cricket. But so much, crammed into so short a time, cloyed the appetite.

At the heart of the debate upon this controversial season and the future pattern of the game in Australia is the question of whether businessmen are necessary for the running of a professional sport. Few people would argue that men of commercial acumen are not required when millions of pounds a year are turned over in the organisation of cricket both in England and in Australia. But the clear danger in Australia, on the evidence of 1979-80, is that businessmen with too little knowledge of cricket and no feeling for the game's spirit and history will shape the sport from a purely commercial point of view to its ultimate detriment.

Bob Parish, the chairman of the Australian Cricket Board, and Lynton Taylor, the boss of PBL, both said at the end of the season that they did not believe the market had been saturated. The former said this to me in an interview only a few minutes after walking up the steps to the commentary box at the Melbourne Cricket Ground after the final Test and remarking as he made his weary way what a 'long, hard season' it had been. Yet he would not admit that almost everyone shared the conclusion implicit in that remark. 'We must give the public what they want,' he kept saying, like a man trying to convince himself. But the public had not asked for the programme which had just been completed. It had been forced upon them. The Channel Nine propagandists had said:

'This is what you will get and you *will* enjoy it.' Some did, some did not, but by the end of the season the uncommitted, convinced by what they were continually told on the television, were saying to themselves: 'It is not quite *my* cup of tea, but it has obviously all been a tremendous success . . . all those brilliant catches and sixes . . . that Viv Richards chap . . . those spectacular fast bowlers . . . the crowds obviously love it.' On the day before I left for England I spoke to one very intelligent person who spoke exactly in these terms. It proves that if a lie is repeated often enough, people will believe it. I doubt if he believed *me* when I told him that Test crowds were down by more than 300,000 compared with five years before. Yet the facts are there, no matter how much PBL and the ACB may wish to view them through rose-coloured, or coloured television, spectacles. The crowds for the six Tests of 1979-80 totalled 437,635. In 1974-75, for the matches against England, they were 776,802. In 1975-76 against West Indies, they were 741,223. Even in 1978-79, when Australia were heavily defeated and when the Tests faced direct rivalry from WSC, crowds totalled 370,592, only 67,000 less than in the 'greatest season ever'. With two very attractive touring teams, mass publicity and intensive promotion, and in the aftermath of the compromise between the warring parties, very much better figures must have been anticipated.

Crowds for the limited-over internationals averaged 19,933 but, as already mentioned, the average night crowd at Sydney was only 15,800. In all, 259,133 people watched the 13 games played. This, certainly, is a healthy number, but what was not calculable was the effect the frequency of big cricket matches was having on the public mind. It is significant that the crowds were biggest for the 'day only' matches at Melbourne and Adelaide, where there was much less one-day cricket than in Sydney. One heard so many people say that they were sick of it all, and that the programme had confused them, that I suspect cricketers were becoming like politicians in election time—meritorious, no doubt, but less and less interesting through being given far too much exposure, and hardly worth turning up to vote for. Absolutely anything in the world can be over-exposed, be it inanimate like the Mona Lisa or animate like the voice of Joan Sutherland. Even Viv Richards becomes ordinary when seen every day of the week.

Though Australia, because of WSC, has been the prime example of the current obsession with 'big match' cricket, it is not the only country where too many international matches are being played too often by the same players. India, for example, toured England between May and September 1979, then without any break played two full series against Australia and Pakistan, and a special Test against England, the 13th of their domestic season. Only a succession of senior players withdrawing persuaded the Indian Board not to undertake a tour of the West Indies early in 1981. The West Indians themselves left Australia to tour New Zealand, then would have played India at home before leaving for a full tour of England. Test matches, and one-day internationals to a lesser extent, make the money to pay the players. But how long before they kill the goose which is laying these golden eggs?

The proliferation of tours really began in the 1970s, as the Australian experience shows. From 1946, when sea travel was still the norm, until 1955-56, only six teams visited Australia in ten years. Three of these were Ashes visits by MCC. Australia made five overseas tours in the decade. In the next, from 1956-57 to 1965-66, the pattern was the same, with six tours to Australia and only four overseas. The proliferation occurred because jet aircraft made travelling so much faster and also no doubt because of the demands of television. Until the sudden increase in matches one heard less about the game's financial problems. Perhaps this was partly because each Test match was a major event, a comparative rarity. It was also, of course, because the expenses of producing cricket were far less, and because of the impact of television, which both draws spectators away and attracts new ones.

The game made radical changes at the start and finish of the 1970s. Since 1970 Australia has had at least one touring team every season: in 1970 MCC, 1971 a Rest of the World XI, 1972 Pakistan, 1973 New Zealand, 1974 England, 1975 West Indies, 1976 Pakistan, 1977 India, 1978 England, and 1979 England *and* West Indies. In the years 1979 and 1980 alone Australia will have played home Test series against England (twice), West Indies, India and New Zealand and will have made tours to India, Pakistan and England (twice again – for the Prudential World Cup and the Centenary Test). So it is not just Australia which is responsible for the overkill.

Nevertheless Australia is leading the way, and despite the warnings of English and Australian cricket writers who were remarkably unanimous in arguing that the 1979-80 programme of six Tests, 15 one-day internationals, 25 Shield games, nine McDonald's Cup one-day games and a limited number of matches between State teams and the two touring sides amounted to an excess, five extra internationals were planned for the following season. The chances are that England will be on a better wicket if they argue for a more traditional tour format in 1982-83 (assuming a postponement of plans to hold a world Test cup in that year) after 1980-81 when New Zealand and India are the less attractive visitors.

In 1979-80 the ACB and PBL made life unnecessarily difficult for themselves by taking on the extra expenses of having two touring teams simultaneously. The obvious alternative was to split the tours, having one team early in the season and the other at the end, with a one-day international tournament in the new year. This would cut expenditure because the tours would be shorter and it would also isolate the limited-over games, allowing the Sheffield Shield greater prominence and the Tests to build their own momentum. Such a system would also be less confusing to spectators and would give players a chance to prepare properly for the type of cricket they were playing, without having constantly to switch from one to the other.

This was the main reason why the 1979-80 experiment was as unsatisfactory for players as it was for spectators. There were many others. Every match tended to be a big match. There was no chance to settle into any rhythm. Pitches were often poor, sometimes because too much cricket was played on tired squares. From the Australian viewpoint, although home players had the advantage of going back into the Sheffield Shield to regain form if they lost their place in the national side, the regular Test players virtually had to forget the Shield, which thus became a second-rate competition for reserves, unpromoted and untelevised (for most of the season). Kim Hughes, for example, did not play one Shield game for Western Australia although he remained fit throughout the season, which he began in India in September and ended in Pakistan in March. Others who went on the tour of India, which had eaten into the first part of the season, also had little

Shield cricket. Yet the Shield has been, and must remain, the breeding-ground of Test players. The less prestige attached to the competition, the smaller inevitably will be the number of quality players coming through.

From the point of view of the two touring teams, the programmes arranged gave little satisfactory preparation for Test cricket. The problem was especially acute for the reserves – men like Stevenson and Larkins for England, and David Murray, Gomes and Marshall for the West Indies. (England at least made more effort than the West Indies to keep their reserves happy and in match practice, but Brearley found this the hardest aspect of the tour, having constantly to disappoint the players on the fringe of the team.) To give but one example, David Bairstow played in only two first-class matches on the whole tour.

Perhaps only the players can effectively withstand the greedy whims of the marketing men and the short-sighted attitude of some administrators. It is for the players to say that there is too much one-day cricket, too many tours, too much travel, and that the trend must stop, even if it means smaller rewards. Their present riches would take longer to acquire, certainly, but their careers would be both longer and more enjoyable.

I have already explained why the Australian players in particular were so weak in accepting a programme which was at least as unfair to themselves as it was to their opponents. They danced like puppets to the tune of PBL – indeed they must have felt Big Brother watching them wherever they went. Every time that an Australian team took the field, at the start of play, after lunch, after tea and *especially* after dinner, they did so to the strains of 'C'mon Aussie C'mon.' At times they must have felt like early commuters arriving at Waterloo station on a wintry Monday morning and being greeted by a strident march coming over the loudspeakers urging them to walk briskly to work when all they really want to do is go back to sleep.

Perhaps I am the only one who was bored by 'C'mon Aussie', undeniably catchy though the tune may be. I doubt, however, if I am alone in considering the much-vaunted promoters of Australian cricket, PBL, unsatisfactory in a number of ways. They gave no discernible promotion to the

raham Dilley, England's youngest Test cricketer for 30 years, showed great
romise. Here he bowls to Greenidge in the one-day finals at Melbourne. Sadly
r England, Bob Willis was out of luck all tour and could find none of his old
ark.

Yorkshire to the fore. *Above* The belligerent Bairstow hits out at Holding in the first of the one-day finals at Melbourne, which West Indies won by 2 runs. *Below* Bairstow and Stevenson race off in jubilation after completing a stunning victory in the last of the one-day games against Australia.

bove Botham's brilliant catching of Ian Chappell in the second innings of the
/dney Test gave Derek Underwood his 100th Test wicket against Australia. But
ngland generally fielded far below their recent standards. *Below* Greg Chappell
cking up a sharp slip catch with typical ease – Willis out to Lillee in the final Test
Melbourne.

Bigger than the game? Ian Chappell (*above*, batting against Underwood in the Sydney Test) and Lillee (*below*, claiming Gower l.b.w. as one of his 11 victims in the Melbourne Test) were undoubted successes on the field, but that they were allowed to play on after well-publicised misdemeanours suggested a ruthless pragmatism on the part of the Australian cricket authorities.

Sheffield Shield or to the early games played by the touring teams. (As mentioned early in the book, exactly eleven spectators watched the players go out for the last morning's play in one of England's early matches.) Neither the major part of the Shield programme nor the few touring matches against the States were televised by PBL's sister company Channel Nine. A final of the McDonald's Cup was played at Sydney for the benefit of television before a minute audience. At Hobart or Perth the match would have had atmosphere, local interest and a decent crowd.

At the grounds themselves, so-called experts made elementary errors over the public address systems. At Melbourne it was announced that the West Indies had defeated Australia in the Test match by 'eleven wickets'. John Lever was frequently called Peter Lever. Bruce Laird was twice called Rick Laird when he walked out to bat at Adelaide. Bob Willis was identified as Derek Underwood, and even when the former put on a special flat-footed Underwood walk the announcer did not seem to realise his mistake. Of course such errors are easily made but there were enough of them to strengthen one's suspicion that the 'promotion' was being handled by people without a deep knowledge of the game and whose main concern was not so much making the game more attractive to the public as attracting the public to the various 'spin-off' sales, like the 'famous Lillee T-shirt' and the 'white cricket balls made of soap' which seemed to be advertised over the public address at every match until the final Test at Melbourne. Perhaps by then they were sold out or the message had got home that all people wanted of a public address system at a cricket match was necessary cricket information.

Spectators were generally given less consideration than, at a minimum entry fee of $A5.50 (£2.25) for any international match, they certainly deserved. At Sydney a high proportion of the Test crowds missed the first hour or so of each day because 21 turnstiles were out of use (due to the rebuilding of the Brewongle Stand) and no attempt was made to provide any temporary ones. The same mistake had been made the season before.

After the last West Indies Test at Adelaide, where quite a large crowd had assembled to see the end of the game on the fifth morning, the Sir Frank Worrell Trophy was presented in the dressing-room by Tony Greig and the crowd were informed that they could see the ceremony on television in the evening. Even the press, normally the first consideration of PR men, were given little consideration. For a long time no TV monitors were available at the SCG and none were provided for any of the ABC commentary boxes.

Another disturbing matter was the failure of Channel Nine to persuade country stations to take their cricket transmissions. Opposition to the Channel Nine takeover of cricket was therefore at its most bitter in country areas. The least attractive part about the promoters, however, was the general impression given by some of their spokesmen and some Channel Nine commentators that Australian cricket had begun to be exciting only when WSC came along. Lynton Taylor was quoted in the *Melbourne Herald* as referring to the 'parlous state of Australian cricket three years ago'. Three years before, the Centenary Test had marked the apogee of the mid-1970s boom in the game in Australia, *the very boom which had first attracted Channel Nine to the game.*

At least in one very important respect, however, the promoters were successful. The upward trend in the figures of people actually playing cricket, which had begun in the early 1970s, continued in 1979-80, according to objective government surveys. Whatever else the pop image of cricket which PBL liked to encourage may have done (and the playing of noisy pop music certainly drove some spectators away) it did not in any way discourage young people from watching and playing the game. Cricket has always attracted the young, but the mass publicity generated by the 1979-80 season seemed genuinely to encourage greater interest amongst children.

Clearly the more the young can be encouraged to play cricket, the healthier the game's future must be. But this in turn makes it all the more vital that the example set at the top should be the right one. One likes to think that the technical expertise of Greg Chappell, Viv Richards and Geoff Boycott will have imprinted itself on young Australian minds. But it is certain that the inspiring brilliance of these players will have been countered to some extent by the occasional examples of player histrionics and hysterical spectators, and also by much of the 'bad' one-day cricket—negative bowling and improvised off-side slogging to counter legside fields. England, who led the way in these tactics but who opposed the original requests for circles, plan to experiment in domestic cricket with an oval-shaped line, which would encourage more attacking bowling without putting spinners at a disadvantage.

Certainly the next generation of Australian cricketers is unlikely to contain many subtle spin bowlers. Only England used them seriously in the one-day games, and in the six Test matches of 1979-80 the spinners took only 26 wickets between them. Almost a decade back, in 1970-71 when John Snow was at his peak and Dennis Lillee was emerging, spinners still took 58 of the 184 wickets in the six completed Tests.

All these matters should be of vital concern to administrators, promoters and players alike if the next generation of professionals is to play cricket to technical and moral standards which are worthy of the game's past. Some would go so far as to say it has no future. One of the greatest of all bowlers, Bill O'Reilly, concluded in the *Sydney Morning Herald*: 'The game as it is will not make it into the 21st century.' This is too alarmist, albeit understandable. Although I personally enjoyed the cricket on this tour less than on previous ones and found the programme too hectic, I think the game is generally healthy. Professional tennis in America, though it has tarnished a good game in some respects because of its obsession with the dollar and a general commercial razzmatazz of the kind which has been applied to cricket in Australia, has resulted in far more tennis being played by far more people. The same may well happen to cricket. But this will only be the case if those who control first-class cricket temper their ambitions with a greater respect for cricket's best traditions and, noting such trends as declining Test crowds, worsening standards of player and crowd behaviour, disappearing spinners and negative tactics, concentrate in future more on quality and less on quantity.

Postscript

BOTHAM'S
JUBILEE EXHIBITION

India's Golden Jubilee Test match, a special match held at the Wankhede Stadium in Bombay to celebrate the fiftieth anniversary of the foundation of the Indian Cricket Board, was both unusual in conception and remarkable in practice. Ian Botham produced one of the greatest individual contributions to any Test in history; Bob Taylor broke a world wicket-keeping record; an umpire twice retracted a decision to give an England batsman out; in a country where draws are frequent, the game ended 25 minutes after lunch on the fourth day; in the land of spin only one wicket in the match was taken by a spinner, and the two specialist spinners picked by England bowled only seven overs in the two Indian innings; and, finally, the rest day was held after only one day's cricket because of an eclipse of the sun.

Overshadowing all, so to speak, was Botham, who eclipsed even the sun. He took 6 for 58 in India's first innings; scored 114, his second successive Test hundred, after England had been 58 for five; and then took 7 for 48 in the second innings. Nobody else has taken more than nine wickets in the same Test as scoring a hundred; nobody else has scored a hundred and taken five or more wickets in a Test innings as often as Botham (he has done so three times in three years, Sobers and Mushtaq Mohammed achieving it twice in their careers); and his match figures of 48.5-14-106-13 have been bettered by only one man in a Test in India, Jusubhai Patel, who took 14 for 124 with off-spin on a newly laid pitch at Kanpur against Australia in 1959.

The pitch, of course, was the key to the records set by Botham and Taylor in the Jubilee Test, which resulted in India's first defeat in an overcrowded season. Earlier they had defeated both Australia (under Kim Hughes) and Pakistan. On a surface which was grassy throughout, the ball moved off the seam and bounced generously. Botham, at medium-fast pace, also made the ball swing consistently.

England, whose selection was shaped partly by injury and illness to Willey, Randall, Dilley and Willis, made two changes in their eleven, Stevenson winning his first Test cap in place of Willis and Emburey coming in for Willey; in the event Emburey went all the way to India in vain, for he was not to bowl a single over before he returned to the Melbourne club from which he had been so hastily summoned on Christmas Day. The selectors again thought hard about bringing in Bairstow for Taylor and the former even came close to playing as a specialist batsman, but in the end he was obliged to spend yet another match as a spectator.

India had only one satisfactory batting session in the game and that was the first of all. After a parade of past Indian players watched by a crowd which only half-filled the stadium (spectators were required to pay £25 for tickets for the whole match—the third Test in Bombay in the same season) India scored 102 for one in an exhilarating start. Gavaskar, in a carefree mood despite having lost the captaincy to Vishwanath, hit 41 of the first 50 scored in only nine overs against bowling from Botham, Lever and Stevenson which tended to be too short. His opening partner, the Anglo-Indian all-rounder Roger Binny, was run out by a brilliant throw from Larkins after making 15 of the opening stand of 56. Gavaskar thereafter went into his shell and was out shortly before lunch, the first of seven men in the match to go down in the scorebook as caught Taylor bowled Botham.

Taylor took another and more difficult catch after lunch, Vengsarkar edging Stevenson well to the wicket-keeper's right to give the Yorkshire all-rounder his first Test wicket. Thereafter it was all Botham and Taylor, with Stevenson and the luckless Lever (who had a number of l.b.w. appeals turned down) occasionally getting into the act in a supporting role. India were bowled out shortly before the close of the first day for 242, despite a typically spirited 40 not out by Syed Kirmani and an innings of 30 by the upstanding and hard-hitting Sandeep Patil, who had only just come into the Test side but who had looked to be something out of the ordinary for a couple of years in Indian domestic cricket. Taylor's seven catches in the first innings equalled the Test record set by

Wasim Bari against New Zealand in Auckland only a year before.

Two more players, who had begun their Test careers in this overcrowded season, the off-spinner Shivlal Yadav and the much more experienced left-arm orthodox spinner Dilip Doshi, had little chance to shine against England. The bulk of the work when play began again after the early rest day was done by the gifted Kapil Dev, the willing Ghavri and the strongly built Binny. At one point this combination had reduced England to an apparently hopeless 58 for five. But England's first-day heroes, Botham and Taylor, now joined formidable forces again and, helped by an outstanding piece of Indian sportsmanship, turned the match irrevocably England's way.

The total was 85 and Taylor had made seven when he played and missed at a ball from Kapil Dev. Kirmani caught the ball and threw it up half-heartedly. A mere glance at the umpire by Kapil Dev was enough to persuade umpire Hanumantha Rao (who had been singled out as an outstandingly promising umpire by Tony Greig's MCC side in 1976-77) to raise his finger with alacrity. No one had seriously appealed and after a surprised pause Taylor moved towards the pavilion, only for Vishwanath to stop him. The new Indian captain walked over to the umpire to withdraw the appeal on the grounds that Taylor had not touched the ball. The umpire asked if this was the view held by all the Indian fielders and after a brief conference in which the former captain Gavaskar played a leading part it was confirmed that this was so. Hanumantha Rao thereupon altered his decision, much to his credit. Oddly enough something similar had happened in the Centenary Test in Australia when Rodney Marsh withdrew an appeal against Derek Randall after Tom Brooks had given him out caught off a scooped half-volley catch. Anniversary matches obviously encourage the perfect sportsmanship and honourable conduct with which cricket has in theory been synonymous. (In the second innings at Bombay umpire Rao gave Boycott out 'caught behind', then quickly retracted his decision when he realised that no one had appealed. Mr Rao, like the players, clearly needed a rest.)

Fortune continued to smile on Taylor, who, when 26, was bowled by a no-ball from Kapil Dev. But the fact is that throughout his time as England's wicket-keeper Taylor, although not recognised as a particularly good batsman, has tended to bat better than he often does for his county. This, indeed, had helped him withstand the challenge to his place from Bairstow. By virtue of concentration and a sound technique he hung on this time whilst Botham, having reached 50 with much greater discretion than he had shown against Australia earlier in the tour, made the second half of another accomplished hundred in seventy minutes with a succession of husky sweeps and powerful drives, many off the back foot. His exhibition was much more generously greeted by the Indian crowd than it would have been at Sydney or Melbourne. The England team certainly noticed this and a few months earlier Kim Hughes had also commented on the Indian crowds' generous appreciation of good cricket, comparing them favourably with the raucous 'one-eyed' masses in his native land.

Botham and Taylor put on 171. Botham's hundred was his sixth in 25 Tests for England. This was double the number of Gower who, during England's earlier collapse, had at least batted with great care before falling l.b.w. Botham was out in the same way to a good ball from Ghavri just before the close of a day which ended with England ten runs behind India with four wickets standing.

This was a fairly balanced position, but by the end of the third day the game was virtually over. More useful batting by Taylor and Lever, and a vigorous 27 not out by Stevenson in his first Test innings, steered England to a lead of 54. Then an Indian team jaded from an excess of Test cricket subsided meekly before the barnstorming Botham. By the end of the day, bowling unchanged with no loss of movement or fire for 24 overs, Botham had taken 6 for 48 and had reduced India to 148 for 8. Gavaskar defended well; Kapil Dev hit some magnificent shots to preserve his reputation as 'the Indian Botham', and Yashpal Sharma held up England for longer than most. But this was about the sum of the serious resistance.

Botham and Lever took the last two wickets early on the fourth morning. Lever moved the ball no less than Botham did but it was the latter's extra bounce which made him the more formidable. All that 'Guy the Gorilla' now had to do was to sit back and watch Boycott and Gooch stroke England to a confident ten-wicket win which ended an often discordant tour on the sweetest possible note.

Earlier Bob Taylor's third catch of the innings, involving a typically nimble and gymnastic dive to his right, had taken his tally to ten in the match, surpassing Gil Langley's record nine for Australia at Lord's in 1956. An Australian comparison is strictly relevant in the final analysis, for the brutal truth is that if this match had been played at Bombay between England and Australia, in conditions well suited to Dennis Lillee, it might have been Rodney Marsh who broke Langley's record and it would almost certainly have been another win for Australia.

The Jubilee Test had merely underlined that the lesson of the 1979-80 season needed desperately to be heeded: too much rich food will satiate even a glutton. International cricket needs to go on to a strict diet, so that every meal is properly appreciated in the future.

INDIA v ENGLAND—Jubilee Test

Bombay, February 15, 17, 18, 19. England won by 10 wickets.

India *First Innings*		*Second Innings*	
S. M. Gavaskar c Taylor b Botham	49	c Taylor b Botham...........	24
R. M. Binny run out	15	lbw b Botham.................	0
D. B. Vengsarkar c Taylor b Stevenson	34	lbw b Lever	10
*G. R. Vishwanath b Lever...............	11	c Taylor b Botham...........	5
S. M. Patil c Taylor b Botham...........	30	lbw b Botham.................	0
Yashpal Sharma lbw b Botham	21	lbw b Botham.................	27
Kapil Dev c Taylor b Botham	0	(8) not out......................	45
†S. M. H. Kirmani not out	40	(7) c Gooch b Botham	0
K. D. Ghavri c Taylor b Stevenson.....	11	c Brearley b Lever	5
Shivlal Yadav c Taylor b Botham	8	c Taylor b Botham...........	15
D. R. Doshi c Taylor b Botham..........	6	c & b Lever	0
Extras (b5, lb3, nb9)........................	17	Extras (b4, lb8, nb5, w1)...	18
Total......................	242	Total	149

Fall of Wickets
1–56 2–102 3–108 4–135 5–160 6–160 7–181 8–197 9–223
1–4 2–22 3–31 4–31 5–56 6–58 7–102 8–115 9–148

Bowling	*First Innings*				*Second Innings*			
Lever	23	3	82	1	20.1	2	65	3
Botham	22.5	7	58	6	26	7	48	7
Stevenson	14	1	59	2	5	1	13	0
Underwood	6	1	23	0	1	0	5	0
Gooch	4	2	3	0				

England *First Innings*		*Second Innings*	
G. A. Gooch c Kirmani b Ghavri........	8	not out..........................	49
G. Boycott c Kirmani b Binny	22	not out..........................	43
W. Larkins lbw b Ghavri..................	0		
D. I. Gower lbw b Kapil Dev.............	16		
*J. M. Brearley lbw b Kapil Dev	5		
I. T. Botham lbw b Ghavri...............	114		
†R. W. Taylor lbw b Kapil Dev	43		
J. E. Emburey c Binny b Ghavri........	8		
J. K. Lever b Doshi........................	21		
G. R. Stevenson not out	27		
D. L. Underwood b Ghavri...............	1		
Extras (b8, lb9, nb14)	31	Extras (b3, lb1, nb2)	6
Total................................	296	Total (no wickets) ..	98

Fall of Wickets
1–21 2–21 3–45 4–57 5–58 6–229 7–245 8–262 9–283

Bowling	*First Innings*				*Second Innings*			
Kapil Dev	29	8	64	3	8	2	21	0
Ghavri	20.1	5	52	5	5	0	12	0
Binny	19	3	70	1				
Doshi	23	6	57	1	6	1	12	0
Yadav	6	2	22	0	6	0	31	0
Patil					3	0	8	0
Gavaskar					1	0	4	0
Vishwanath					0.3	0	4	0

Toss won by India
Man of the Match: I. T. Botham
Umpires: G. D. Ghosh and S. N. Hanumantha Rao

A Statistical Survey

Compiled by Patrick Allen

(1) THE TEAMS

England Touring Team to Australia

BREARLEY, John Michael (Captain)	Middlesex	28 April 1942
WILLIS, Robert George Dylan		
(Vice-Captain)	Warwickshire	30 May 1949
BAIRSTOW, David Leslie	Yorkshire	1 September 1951
BOTHAM, Ian Terrence	Somerset	24 November 1955
BOYCOTT, Geoffrey	Yorkshire	21 October 1940
DILLEY, Graham Roy	Kent	18 May 1959
EMBUREY, John Ernest	Middlesex	20 August 1952
GOOCH, Graham Alan	Essex	23 July 1953
GOWER, David Ivon	Leicestershire	1 April 1957
HENDRICK, Michael	Derbyshire	22 October 1948
LARKINS, Wayne	Northamptonshire	22 November 1953
LEVER, John Kenneth	Essex	24 February 1949
MILLER, Geoffrey	Derbyshire	8 September 1952
RANDALL, Derek William	Nottinghamshire	24 February 1951
STEVENSON, Graham Barry	Yorkshire	16 December 1955
TAYLOR, Robert William	Derbyshire	17 July 1941
UNDERWOOD, Derek Leslie	Kent	8 June 1945
WILLEY, Peter	Northamptonshire	6 December 1949
BEDSER, Alec Victor (Manager)	ex-Surrey	4 July 1918
BARRINGTON, Kenneth Frank		
(Assistant Manager)	ex-Surrey	24 November 1930
THOMAS, Bernard (Physiotherapist)		

G. B. Stevenson replaced M. Hendrick, who returned home due to a shoulder injury (November 26).

J.E. Emburey replaced G. Miller, who returned home with a back injury (December 25).

West Indies Touring Team to Australia

LLOYD, Clive Hubert (Captain)	Guyana and Lancashire	31 August 1944
MURRAY, Deryck Lance		
(Vice-Captain)	Trinidad	20 May 1943
CROFT, Colin Everton Hunte	Guyana	15 March 1953
GARNER, Joel	Barbados and Somerset	12 December 1952
GOMES, Hilary Angelo	Trinidad	13 July 1953

145

GREENIDGE, Cuthbert Gordon	Barbados and Hampshire	2 May 1951
HAYNES, Desmond Leo	Barbados	15 February 1956
HOLDING, Michael Anthony	Jamaica	16 February 1954
KALLICHARRAN, Alvin Isaac	Guyana and Warwickshire	21 March 1949
KING, Collis Llewellyn	Barbados	11 June 1951
MARSHALL, Michael Denzil	Barbados and Hampshire	18 April 1958
MURRAY, David Anthony	Barbados	29 May 1950
PARRY, Derek Ricaldo	Combined Islands	22 December 1954
RICHARDS, Isaac Vivian Alexander	Combined Islands and Somerset	7 March 1952
ROBERTS, Anderson Montgomery Everton	Combined Islands	29 January 1951
ROWE, Lawrence George	Jamaica	8 January 1949
RODRIGUES, William Vincente (Manager)	ex-Trinidad	25 June 1934

Australian players for Test & One-Day International Matches

*CHAPPELL, Gregory Stephen (Captain)	Queensland	7 August 1948
BORDER, Allan Robert	New South Wales	27 July 1955
*BRIGHT, Raymond James	Victoria	13 July 1954
*CHAPPELL, Ian Michael	South Australia	29 September 1943
DARLING, Warrick Maxwell	South Australia	1 May 1957
DYMOCK, Geoffrey	Queensland	21 July 1945
HIGGS, James Donald	Victoria	15 July 1950
HOGG, Rodney Malcolm	South Australia	5 March 1951
*HOOKES, David William	South Australia	3 May 1955
HUGHES, Kimberley John	Western Australia	26 January 1954
*LAIRD, Bruce Malcolm	Western Australia	21 November 1950
LAUGHLIN, Trevor John	Victoria	30 January 1951
*LILLEE, Dennis Keith	Western Australia	18 July 1949
*MALLETT, Ashley Alexander	South Australia	13 July 1945
*MARSH, Rodney William	Western Australia	11 November 1947
*McCOSKER, Richard Bede	New South Wales	11 December 1946
*PASCOE, Leonard Stephen	New South Wales	13 February 1950
THOMSON, Jeffrey Robert	Queensland	16 August 1950
TOOHEY, Peter Michael	New South Wales	20 April 1954
*WALKER, Maxwell Henry Norman	Victoria	12 September 1948
*WALTERS, Kevin Douglas	New South Wales	21 December 1945
WHATMORE, Davenall Frederick	Victoria	16 March 1954
WIENER, Julien Mark	Victoria	1 May 1955
YALLOP, Graham Neil	Victoria	7 October 1952

*Asterisk indicates those players formerly employed by World Series Cricket

(2) THE RESULTS

Match record of official MCC teams in Australia

Season	Captain	P	First-class matches			
			W	D	L	T
1903–04	P. F. Warner	14	9	3	2	—
1907–08	A. O. Jones	18	7	7	4	—
1911–12	J. W. H. T. Douglas	14	11	2	1	—
1920–21	J. W. H. T. Douglas	13	5	2	6	—
1922–23	A. C. MacLaren	7	0	4	3	—
1924–25	A. E. R. Gilligan	17	7	4	6	—
1928–29	A. P. F. Chapman	17	8	8	1	—
1929–30	A. H. H. Gilligan	5	2	1	2	—
1932–33	D. R. Jardine	17	10	5	1	1
1935–36	E. R. T. Holmes	6	3	2	1	—
1936–37	G. O. B. Allen	17	5	7	5	—
1946–47	W. R. Hammond	17	1	13	3	—
1950–51	F. R. Brown	16	5	7	4	—
1954–55	L Hutton	17	8	7	2	—
1958–59	P. B. H. May	17	4	9	4	—
1962–63	E. R. Dexter	15	4	8	3	—
1965–66	M. J. K. Smith	15	5	8	2	—
1970–71	R. Illingworth	14	3	10	1	—
1974–75	M. H. Denness	15	5	5	5	—
1977	A. W. Greig	2	0	1	1	—
1978–79	J. M. Brearley	13	8	3	2	—
1979–79	J. M. Brearley	8	3	2	3	—
TOTALS		294	113	118	62	1

Australia v England—in Australia

Series	P	Tests			Adelaide			Brisbane			Melbourne			Perth			Sydney		
		E	A	D	E	A	D	E	A	D	E	A	D	E	A	D	E	A	D
1876–77	2	1	1	—	—	—	—	—	—	—	1	1	—	—	—	—	—	—	—
1878–79	1	—	1	—	—	—	—	—	—	—	—	1	—	—	—	—	—	—	—
1881–82	4	—	2	2	—	—	—	—	—	—	—	—	2	—	—	—	—	2	—
1882–83	4	2	2	—	—	—	—	—	—	—	1	1	—	—	—	—	1	1	—
1884–85	5	3	2	—	1	—	—	—	—	—	2	—	—	—	—	—	—	2	—
1886–87	2	2	—	—	—	—	—	—	—	—	—	—	—	—	—	—	2	—	—
1887–88	1	1	—	—	—	—	—	—	—	—	—	—	—	—	—	—	1	—	—
1891–92	3	1	2	—	1	—	—	—	—	—	—	1	—	—	—	—	—	1	—
1894–95	5	3	2	—	—	1	—	—	—	—	2	—	—	—	—	—	1	1	—
1897–98	5	1	4	—	—	1	—	—	—	—	—	2	—	—	—	—	1	1	—
1901–02	5	1	4	—	—	1	—	—	—	—	—	2	—	—	—	—	1	1	—
1903–04	5	3	2	—	—	1	—	—	—	—	1	1	—	—	—	—	2	—	—
1907–08	5	1	4	—	—	1	—	—	—	—	1	1	—	—	—	—	—	2	—
1911–12	5	4	1	—	1	—	—	—	—	—	2	—	—	—	—	—	1	1	—
1920–21	5	—	5	—	—	1	—	—	—	—	—	2	—	—	—	—	—	2	—
1924–25	5	1	4	—	—	1	—	—	—	—	1	1	—	—	—	—	—	2	—
1928–29	5	4	1	—	1	—	—	1	—	—	1	1	—	—	—	—	1	—	—
1932–33	5	4	1	—	1	—	—	1	—	—	—	1	—	—	—	—	2	—	—
1936–37	5	2	3	—	—	1	—	1	—	—	—	2	—	—	—	—	1	—	—
1946–47	5	—	3	2	—	—	1	—	1	—	—	—	1	—	—	—	—	2	—
1950–51	5	1	4	—	—	1	—	—	1	—	1	1	—	—	—	—	—	1	—
1954–55	5	3	1	1	1	—	—	—	1	—	1	—	—	—	—	—	1	—	1
1958–59	5	—	4	1	—	1	—	—	1	—	—	2	—	—	—	—	—	—	1
1962–63	5	1	1	3	—	—	1	—	—	1	1	—	—	—	—	—	1	1	1
1965–66	5	1	1	3	—	1	—	—	—	1	—	—	2	—	—	—	1	—	—
1970–71	6	2	—	4	—	—	1	—	—	1	—	—	1	—	—	1	2	—	—
1974–75	6	1	4	1	—	1	—	—	1	—	1	—	1	—	1	1	—	1	—
1977	1	—	1	—	—	—	—	—	—	—	—	1	—	—	—	—	—	—	—
1978–79	6	5	1	—	1	—	—	1	—	—	—	1	—	1	—	—	2	—	—
1979–80	3	0	3	—	—	—	—	—	—	—	—	1	—	—	1	—	—	1	—
TOTALS	129	48	64	17	7	12	3	4	5	3	16	23	7	1	2	2	20	22	3

147

(3) THE SCORES

ENGLAND IN AUSTRALIA: matches other than Tests and One-Day Internationals

Brisbane. November 12, 13, 14. Match drawn.
England XI 176 (D. W. Randall 97, C. G. Rackemann 5 for 25) and 226 for 5 dec. (P. Willey 57*, G. Miller 57*, D. I. Gower 50)
Queensland 219 for 9 dec. (T. V. Hohns 62, M. F. Kent 58, G. J. Cosier 43) and 97 for 1 (G. S. Chappell 49*)

Newcastle. November 17. England XI won by 9 wickets (not first-class).
Northern NSW 133 (48 overs) (C. Beatty 67)
England XI 136 for 1 (43 overs) (G. Boycott 78)

Newcastle. November 18. England XI won by 32 runs (not first-class).
England XI 213 for 7 (50 overs) (J. M. Brearley 67, W. Larkins 51)
Northern NSW 181 for 7 (50 overs) (G. G. Geise 58*)

Adelaide. November 22, 23, 24, 25. Match drawn (not first-class).
England XI 179 (D. W. Randall 61, G. Kirkwood 5 for 52) and 411 for 8 dec. (G. A. Gooch 124, I. T. Botham 76, R. W. Taylor 66*, G. Boycott 41, G. Kirkwood 4 for 96)
Combined Universities 168 (C. Beatty 53, D. L. Underwood 8 for 41) and 227 for 5 (D. Wellham 95, P. J. Davies 57)

Hobart. November 30, December 1, 2. England XI won by 100 runs.
England XI 214 for 3 dec. (G. Boycott 101*, G. A. Gooch 51) and 135 for 1 dec. (G. A. Gooch 70*, D. I. Gower 53)
Tasmania 71 for 3 dec. and 178 (R. L. Knight 74, D. L. Underwood 7 for 66)

Adelaide. December 4, 5, 6. Match drawn.
England XI 252 for 2 dec. (G. Boycott 110, J. M. Brearley 81) and 227 for 7 dec. (G. Miller 71, G. Boycott 63*)
South Australia 226 for 4 dec. (J. J. Crowe 78*, J. E. Nash 48, W. M. Darling 45) and 181 for 3 (W. M. Darling 75*, J. J. Crowe 55)

Brisbane. December 28, 29, 30, 31. England XI won by 138 runs
England XI 324 (G. A. Gooch 115, J. E. Emburey 50) and 274 for 8 dec. (P. Willey 101*, G. A. Gooch 53, D. W. Randall 42)
Queensland 237 (W. R. Broad 53, A. D. Parker 52*, W. G. Morgan 50) and 223 (W. R. Broad 45, A. D. Ogilvie 42)

Canberra. January 27, 28, 29. England XI won by 8 wickets.
New South Wales 212 for 7 dec. (K. D. Walters 62, G. B. Stevenson 4 for 44) and 243 for 2 dec. (A. M. J. Hilditch 78, T. M. Chappell 70*, J. Dyson 45)
England XI 203 (R. W. Taylor 47*, D. W. Randall 44) and 254 for 2 (W. Larkins 90, G. A. Gooch 73*, G. Boycott 51)

WEST INDIES IN AUSTRALIA: matches other than Tests and One-Day Internationals

Geelong. November 11, 12, 13. Match drawn (not first-class).
West Indians 224 (D. L. Haynes 64) and 132 for 3 (D. L. Haynes 59)
Geelong & Districts 227 (P. Caulfield 68, P. Marshall 48, M. D. Marshall 5 for 62, C. E. H. Croft 4 for 49)

Adelaide. November 16, 17, 18. West Indians won by 9 wickets.
South Australia 202 (W. M. Darling 88, M. A. Holding 4 for 27, J. Garner 4 for 73) and 233 (D. W. Hookes 67, T. J. Robertson 40*, A. M. E. Roberts 4 for 25)
West Indians 397 (D. L. Murray 103, I. V. A. Richards 79, D. L. Haynes 58, C. G. Greenidge 45, R. M. Hogg 6 for 95) and 42 for 1

Devonport. November 23, 24, 25. West Indians won by 260 runs.
West Indians 374 (I. V. A. Richards 127, A. I. Kallicharran 123) and 202 for 4 dec. (H. A. Gomes 64*, C. L. King 41)
Invitation XI 144 (C. E. H. Croft 5 for 49) and 172 (R. L. Knight 57, G. J. Cosier 49, J. Garner 4 for 59)

Yea. December 11. Match drawn (not first-class).
West Indians 329 for 3 dec. (L. G. Rowe 97, C. G. Greenidge 77, D. L. Haynes 74, H. A. Gomes 55*)
Victorian Country XI 133 for 8 (D. R. Parry 4 for 21)

Launceston. December 14, 15, 16, 17. West Indians won by an innings and 61 runs.
Tasmania 213 (D. C. Boon 78, C. E. H. Croft 5 for 65) and 271 (R. D. Woolley 93, J. Garner 5 for 43)
West Indians 545 for 5 dec. (A. I. Kallicharran 138, H. A. Gomes 137*, L. G. Rowe 82, C. H. Lloyd 77, D. L. Murray 44*)

Toowoomba. December 19. West Indians won by 4 wickets and continued batting (not first-class).
Queensland Country XI 96
West Indians 124 for 7 (C. L. King 56)

Perth. January 5, 6, 7. Western Australia won by 8 wickets.
West Indians 169 (T. M. Alderman 5 for 47, M. F. Malone 4 for 48) and 313 (C. L. King 92, D. R. Parry 41, A. I. Kallicharran 40)
Western Australia 396 for 6 dec. (R. S. Langer 137, K. S. McEwan 112, A. L. Mann 56*) and 87 for 2 (G. Shipperd 44)

Perth. January 8. West Indians won by 4 wickets (not first-class).
Western Australia 223 for 8 (50 overs) (R. S. Langer 47, G. M. Wood 43)
West Indians 224 for 6 (49.1 overs) (A. I. Kallicharran 77, D. L. Haynes 60, C. G. Greenidge 51, G. D. Porter 4 for 49)

Canberra. January 14. West Indians won by 121 runs (not first-class).
West Indians 261 for 4 (50 overs) (L. G. Rowe 88*, C. G. Greenidge 57, D. L. Haynes 50)
Australian Capital Territory 140 for 9 (50 overs)

THE TEST MATCHES

AUSTRALIA v WEST INDIES—First Test Match

Brisbane. December 1, 2, 3, 4, 5. Match drawn.

Australia *First Innings*

B. M. Laird c Murray b Garner	92	
R. B. McCosker c Kallicharran b Croft	14	
A. R. Border c Murray b Garner	1	
*G. S. Chappell c King b Roberts	74	
K. J. Hughes b Croft	3	
D. W. Hookes c Holding b Croft	43	
†R. W. Marsh c Murray b Garner	3	
R. J. Bright b Holding	13	
D. K. Lillee lbw b Garner	0	
R. M. Hogg b Roberts	8	
J. R. Thomson not out	0	
Extras (b1, lb4, nb12)	17	
Total	268	

Second Innings

c sub (Marshall) b Garner	75
b Holding	33
c Richards b Garner	7
b Croft	124
not out	130
b Roberts	37
c Kallicharran b King	19
not out	2
Extras (b2, lb11, w2, nb6)	21
Total (6 wickets dec.)	448

Fall of Wickets:
1–19 2–26 3–156 4–174 5–228 6–242 7–246 8–252 9–268
1–40 2–55 3–179 4–297 5–371 6–442

Bowling	First Innings				Second Innings			
Roberts	18.1	5	50	2	27	5	70	1
Holding	16	3	53	1	30	4	94	1
Croft	25	6	80	3	28	3	106	1
Garner	22	5	55	4	41	13	75	2
King	5	1	13	0	22	6	50	1
Kallicharran					18	2	32	0

West Indies *First Innings*

D. L Haynes c Marsh b Thomson	42	
C. G. Greenidge c Marsh b Lillee	34	
I. V. A. Richards c Marsh b Lillee	140	
A. I. Kallicharran c Marsh b Thomson	38	
L. G. Rowe b Chappell	50	
C. L. King c Marsh b Lillee	0	
*†D. L. Murray c McCosker b Thomson	21	
A. M. E. Roberts run out	7	
J. Garner lbw b Lillee	60	
M. A. Holding b Bright	11	
C. E. H. Croft not out	2	
Extras (b5, lb3, nb28)	36	
Total	441	

Second Innings

lbw b Hogg	4
c McCosker b Thomson	0
not out	10
(3) b Hogg	3
(5) not out	8
Extras (b5, w1, nb9)	15
Total (3 wickets)	40

Fall of Wickets:
1–68 2–93 3–198 4–317 5–317 6–341 7–365 8–366 9–385
1–2 2–15 3–16

Bowling	First Innings				Second Innings			
Lillee	29.1	8	104	4	2	0	3	0
Hogg	25	6	55	0	5	2	11	2
Thomson	24	4	90	3	3	2	3	1
Bright	32	9	97	1	4	3	8	0
Chappell	12	2	25	1				
Border	5	1	19	0				
Hookes	5	2	15	0				

Toss won by West Indies
Man of the Match: I. V. A. Richards
Umpires: R. C. Bailhache and A. R. Crafter

AUSTRALIA v WEST INDIES—Second Test Match

Melbourne. December 29, 30, 31, January 1. West Indies won by 10 wickets.

Australia *First Innings*

J. M. Wiener lbw b Garner	40	
B. M. Laird c Lloyd b Holding	16	
A. R. Border c Richards b Garner	17	
*G. S. Chappell c Murray b Garner	19	
K. J. Hughes c Rowe b Holding	4	
P. M. Toohey c Roberts b Holding	10	
†R. W. Marsh c Kallicharran b Holding	0	
D. K. Lillee c Lloyd b Croft	12	
G. Dymock c Kallicharran b Croft	7	
R. M. Hogg c Greenidge b Croft	14	
J. D. Higgs not out	0	
Extras (b9, lb4, w2, nb2)	17	
Total	156	

Second Innings

c Murray b Croft	24
c Garner b Holding	69
lbw b Holding	15
c Murray b Roberts	22
lbw b Roberts	70
c Murray b Croft	7
b Croft	7
c & b Roberts	0
c Lloyd b Garner	17
c Holding b Garner	11
not out	0
Extras (b2, lb10, nb5)	17
Total	259

Fall of Wickets:
1–38 2–69 3–97 4–108 5–112 6–118 7–123 8–133 9–143
1–43 2–88 3–121 4–187 5–205 6–228 7–228 8–233 9–258

Bowling	First Innings				Second Innings			
Roberts	14	1	39	0	21	1	64	3
Holding	14	3	40	4	23	7	61	2
Croft	13.3	4	27	3	22	2	61	3
Garner	15	7	33	3	20.4	2	56	2

West Indies *First Innings*

C. G. Greenidge c Higgs b Dymock	48	
D. L. Haynes c Hughes b Lillee	29	
I. V. A. Richards c Toohey b Dymock	96	
A. I. Kallicharran c Laird b Higgs	39	
L. G. Rowe b Lillee	26	
*C. H. Lloyd c Marsh b Dymock	40	
†D. L. Murray b Dymock	24	
A. M. E. Roberts lbw b Lillee	54	
J. Garner c Dymock b Higgs	29	
M. A. Holding not out	1	
C. E. H. Croft lbw b Higgs	0	
Extras (lb4, nb7)	11	
Total	397	

Second Innings

not out	9
not out	9
Extras (lb4)	4
Total (for 0 wicket)	22

Fall of Wickets:
1–46 2–156 3–215 4–226 5–250 6–305 7–320 8–390 9–396

Bowling	First Innings				Second Innings			
Lillee	*36	7	96	3	3	0	9	0
Hogg	6	0	59	0				
Dymock	31	2	106	4	3	0	5	0
Higgs	34.4	4	122	3				
Chappell	5	2	3	0				
Hughes					1	1	0	0
Toohey					0.2	0	4	0

Toss won by Australia
Man of the Match: I. V. A. Richards
Umpires: A. R. Crafter and C. E. Harvey

AUSTRALIA v WEST INDIES—Third Test Match

Adelaide. January 26, 27, 28, 29, 30. West Indies won by 408 runs.

West Indies *First Innings*

		Second Innings	
C. G. Greenidge lbw b Lillee	6	st Marsh b Mallett	76
D. L. Haynes c Lillee b Mallett	28	c Marsh b Pascoe	27
I. V. A. Richards c Marsh b Lillee	76	b Border	74
A. I. Kallicharran c I. Chappell b Mallett	9	b Mallett	106
L. G. Rowe c Lillee b Dymock	40	c Marsh b Dymock	43
*C. H. Lloyd lbw b Lillee	121	(7) c Marsh b Dymock	40
†D. L. Murray c Marsh b Dymock	4	(8) c G. Chappell b Dymock	28
A. M. E. Roberts b Lillee	9	(9) c Laird b Dymock	8
J. Garner c Hughes b Lillee	16	(10) not out	1
M. A. Holding b Pascoe	9	(11) lbw b Dymock	1
C. E. H. Croft not out	1	(6) c Border b Pascoe	12
Extras (b2, nb7)	9	Extras (b1, 1b10, nb21)	32
Total	328	Total	448

Fall of Wickets

1–11 2–115 3–115 4–126 5–239 6–252 7–300 8–303 9–326
1–48 2–184 3–213 4–299 5–331 6–398 7–417 8–443 9–446

Bowling	First Innings				Second Innings			
Lillee	24	3	78	5	26	6	75	0
Dymock	25	7	74	2	33.5	7	104	5
Pascoe	15.3	1	90	1	25	3	93	2
Mallett	27	5	77	2	38	7	134	2
Border					4	2	10	1

Australia *First Innings*

		Second Innings	
J. M. Wiener c Haynes b Holding	3	c Murray b Roberts	8
B. M. Laird c Garner b Croft	52	lbw b Garner	36
I. M. Chappell c Greenidge b Roberts	2	c Murray b Holding	4
*G. S. Chappell c Garner b Roberts	0	lbw b Croft	31
K. J. Hughes c Lloyd b Croft	34	lbw b Garner	11
A. R. Border b Roberts	54	c Greenidge b Roberts	24
†R. W. Marsh c Murray b Croft	5	not out	23
D. K. Lillee c Haynes b Holding	16	c Kallicharran b Croft	0
G. Dymock c Rowe b Croft	10	c Richards b Holding	2
A. A. Mallett c Rowe b Garner	0	b Holding	5
L. S. Pascoe not out	5	b Holding	5
Extras (b1, 1b14, nb7)	22	Extras (1b2, w2, nb5)	9
Total	203	Total	165

Fall of Wickets

1–23 2–26 3–26 4–83 5–110 6–127 7–165 8–188 9–189
1–12 2–21 3–71 4–83 5–98 6–130 7–131 8–135 9–159

Bowling	First Innings				Second Innings			
Roberts	16.5	3	43	3	15	5	30	2
Holding	15	5	31	2	13	2	40	4
Garner	18	4	43	1	11	3	39	2
Richards	2	0	7	0				
Croft	22	4	57	4	11	1	47	2

Toss won by Australia
Man of the Match: C. H. Lloyd
Umpires: M. W. Johnson and M. G. O'Connell

AUSTRALIA v ENGLAND—First Test Match

Perth. December 14, 15, 16, 18, 19. Australia won by 138 runs.

Australia *First Innings*

			Second Innings	
J. M. Wiener run out	11		c Randall b Underwood	58
B. M. Laird lbw b Botham	0		c Taylor b Underwood	33
A. R. Border lbw b Botham	4		c Taylor b Willis	115
*G. S. Chappell c Boycott b Botham	19		st Taylor b Underwood	43
K. J. Hughes c Brearley b Underwood	99		c Miller b Botham	4
P. M. Toohey c Underwood b Dilley	19		c Taylor b Botham	3
†R. W. Marsh c Taylor b Dilley	42		c Gower b Botham	4
R. J. Bright c Taylor b Botham	17		lbw b Botham	12
D. K. Lillee c Taylor b Botham	18		c Willey b Dilley	19
G. Dymock b Botham	5		not out	20
J. R. Thomson not out	1		b Botham	8
Extras (b4, lb3, nb2)	9		Extras (b4, lb5, w2, nb7)	18
Total	244		Total	337

Fall of Wickets

1–2 2–17 3–20 4–88 5–127 6–186 7–219 8–219 9–243

1–91 2–100 3–168 4–183 5–191 6–204 7–225 8–303 9–323

Bowling	First Innings				Second Innings			
Dilley	18	1	47	2	18	3	50	1
Botham	35	9	78	6	45.5	14	98	5
Willis	23	7	47	0	26	7	52	1
Underwood	13	4	33	1	41	14	82	3
Miller	11	2	30	0	10	0	36	0
Willey					1	0	1	0

England *First Innings*

			Second Innings	
D. W. Randall c Hughes b Lillee	0		lbw b Dymock	1
G. Boycott lbw b Lillee	0		not out	99
P. Willey c Chappell b Dymock	9		lbw b Dymock	12
D. I. Gower c Marsh b Lillee	17		c Thomson b Dymock	23
G. Miller c Hughes b Thomson	25		c Chappell b Thomson	8
*J. M. Brearley c Marsh b Lillee	64		(7) c Marsh b Bright	11
I. T. Botham c Toohey b Thomson	15		(6) c Marsh b Lillee	18
†R. W. Taylor b Chappell	14		b Lillee	15
G. R. Dilley not out	38		c Marsh b Dymock	16
D. L. Underwood lbw b Dymock	13		c Wiener b Dymock	0
R. G. D. Willis b Dymock	11		c Chappell b Dymock	0
Extras (lb7, nb15)	22		Extras (w1, lb3, nb8)	12
Total	228		Total	215

Fall of Wickets:

1–1 2–12 3–14 4–41 5–74 6–90 7–123 8–185 9–203

1–8 2–26 3–64 4–75 5–115 6–141 7–182 8–211 9–211

Bowling	First Innings				Second Innings			
Lillee	28	11	73	4	23	5	74	2
Dymock	29.1	14	52	3	17.2	4	34	6
Chappell	11	6	5	1	6	4	6	0
Thomson	21	3	70	2	11	3	30	1
Bright	2	0	6	0	23	11	30	1
Wiener					8	3	22	0
Border					2	0	7	0

Toss won by England
Man of the Match: I. T. Botham
Umpires: M. G. O'Connell and D. G. Weser

AUSTRALIA v ENGLAND—Second Test Match

Sydney. January 4, 5, 6, 8. Australia won by 6 wickets.

England *First Innings*

		Second Innings	
G. A. Gooch b Lillee	18	c G. S. Chappell b Dymock	4
G. Boycott b Dymock	8	c McCosker b Pascoe	18
D. W. Randall c G. S. Chappell b Lillee	0	(6) c Marsh b G. S. Chappell	25
P. Willey c Wiener b Dymock	8	(3) b Pascoe	3
*J. M. Brearley c Pascoe b Dymock	7	(4) c Marsh b Pascoe	19
D. I. Gower b G. S. Chappell	3	(7) not out	98
I. T. Botham c G. S. Chappell b Pascoe	27	(8) c Wiener b G. S. Chappell	0
†R. W. Taylor c Marsh b Lillee	10	(9) b Lillee	8
G. R. Dilley not out	22	(10) b Dymock	4
R. G. D. Willis c Wiener b Dymock	3	(11) c G. S. Chappell b Lillee	1
D. L. Underwood c Border b Lillee	12	(5) c Border b Dymock	43
Extras (nb5)	5	Extras (b1, lb10, nb2, w1)	14
Total	123	Total	237

Fall of Wickets:
1-10 2-13 3-31 4-38 5-41 6-74 7-75 8-90 9-98
1-6 2-21 3-29 4-77 5-105 6-156 7-174 8-211 9-218

Bowling	*First Innings*				*Second Innings*			
Lillee	13.3	4	40	4	24.3	6	63	2
Dymock	17	6	42	4	28	8	48	3
Pascoe	9	4	14	1	23	3	76	3
G. S. Chappell	4	1	19	1	21	10	36	2
Higgs	1	0	3	0				

Australia *First Innings*

		Second Innings	
R. B. McCosker c Gower b Willis	1	(2) c Taylor b Underwood	41
J. M. Wiener run out	22	(1) b Underwood	13
I. M. Chappell c Brearley b Gooch	42	c Botham b Underwood	9
*G. S. Chappell c Taylor b Underwood	3	not out	98
K. J. Hughes c Taylor b Botham	18	c Dilley b Willis	47
A. R. Border c Gooch b Botham	15	not out	2
†R. W. Marsh c Underwood b Gooch	7		
D. K. Lillee c Brearley b Botham	5		
G. Dymock c Taylor b Botham	4		
L. S. Pascoe not out	10		
J. D. Higgs b Underwood	2		
Extras (b2, lb12, w2)	16	Extras (lb8, w1)	9
Total	145	Total (4 wickets)	219

Fall of Wickets:
1-18 2-52 3-71 4-92 5-100 6-114 7-121 8-129 9-132
1-31 2-51 3-98 4-203

Bowling	*First Innings*				*Second Innings*			
Botham	17	7	29	4	23.3	12	43	0
Willis	11	3	30	1	12	2	26	1
Underwood	13.2	3	39	2	26	6	71	3
Dilley	5	1	13	0	12	0	33	0
Willey	1	0	2	0	4	0	17	0
Gooch	11	4	16	2	8	2	20	0

Toss won by Australia
Man of the Match: G. S. Chappell
Umpires: R. C. Bailhache and W. J. Copeland

AUSTRALIA v ENGLAND—Third Test Match

Melbourne. February 1, 2, 3, 5, 6. Australia won by 8 wickets.

England *First Innings*

		Second Innings	
G. A. Gooch run out	99	b Mallett	51
G. Boycott c Mallett b Dymock	44	b Lillee	7
W. Larkins c G. Chappell b Pascoe	25	lbw b Pascoe	3
D. I. Gower lbw b Lillee	0	b Lillee	11
P. Willey lbw b Pascoe	1	c Marsh b Lillee	2
I. T. Botham c Marsh b Lillee	8	(7) not out	119
*J. M. Brearley not out	60	(6) c Border b Pascoe	10
†R. W. Taylor b Lillee	23	c Border b Lillee	32
D. L. Underwood c I. Chappell b Lillee	3	b Pascoe	0
J. K. Lever b Lillee	22	c Marsh b Lillee	12
R. G. D. Willis c G. Chappell b Lillee	4	c G. Chappell b Pascoe	2
Extras (b1, lb2 nb14)	17	Extras (b2, lb12, nb10)	24
Total	306	Total	273

Fall of Wickets:
1–116 2–170 3–175 4–177 5–177 6–192 7–238 8–242 9–296
1–25 2–46 3–64 4–67 5–88 6–92 7–178 8–179 9–268

Bowling	First Innings				Second Innings			
Lillee	33.1	9	60	6	33	6	78	5
Dymock	28	6	54	1	11	2	30	0
Mallett	35	9	104	0	14	1	45	1
Pascoe	32	7	71	2	29.5	3	80	4
Border					4	0	16	0

Australia *First Innings*

		Second Innings	
R. B. McCosker c Botham b Underwood	33	lbw b Botham	2
B. M. Laird c Gower b Underwood	74	c Boycott b Underwood	25
I. M. Chappell c & b Underwood	75	not out	26
K. J. Hughes c Underwood b Botham	15		
A. R. Border c & b Lever	63		
*G. S. Chappell c Larkins b Lever	114	(4) not out	40
†R. W. Marsh c Botham b Lever	17		
D. K. Lillee c Willey b Lever	8		
G. Dymock b Botham	19		
A. A. Mallett lbw b Botham	25		
L. S. Pascoe not out	1		
Extras (b13, lb12, nb7, w1)	33	Extras (lb8, nb2)	10
Total	477	Total (2 wickets)	103

Fall of Wickets:
1–52 2–179 3–196 4–219 5–345 6–411 7–421 8–432 9–465
1–20 2–42

Bowling	First Innings				Second Innings			
Lever	53	15	111	4	7.4	3	18	0
Botham	39.5	15	105	3	12	5	18	1
Willis	21	4	61	0	5	3	8	0
Underwood	53	19	131	3	14	2	49	1
Willey	13	2	36	0				

Toss won by England
Man of the Match: D. K. Lillee
Umpires: R. C. Bailhache and P. M. Cronin

BENSON & HEDGES WORLD SERIES CUP
First Australia v West Indies Match
Sydney, November 27 (Australia won by 5 wickets)
West Indies

C. G. Greenidge b Lillee	5
D. L. Haynes b Border	29
I. V. A. Richards lbw b Lillee	9
A. I. Kallicharran c & b Border	49
*C. H. Lloyd c Marsh b Border	16
C. L. King b Pascoe	29
†D. L. Murray b Pascoe	27
A. M. E. Roberts b Pascoe	16
J. Garner run out	5
M. A. Holding c McCosker b Pascoe	2
C. E. H. Croft not out	0
Extras (lb3, nb3)	6
(49.3 overs)	193

Fall of Wickets:
1–6 2–18 3–89 4–112 5–117 6–164 7–177 8–187 9–193

Bowling				
Lillee	6	2	10	2
Pascoe	9.3	1	29	4
Bright	5	0	26	0
Hogg	10	0	49	0
Border	10	0	36	3
Chappell	9	0	37	0

Australia

B. M. Laird b Croft	20
R. B. McCosker lbw b Holding	1
A. R. Border c Murray b Croft	17
*G. S. Chappell not out	74
K. J. Hughes b Richards	52
D. W. Hookes b Richards	0
†R. W. Marsh not out	18
Extras (lb14)	14
(47.1 overs) (5 wickets)	196

Did not bat: R. J. Bright, D. K. Lillee, R. M. Hogg and L. R. Pascoe

Fall of Wickets:
1–1 2–37 3–52 4–144 5–144

Bowling				
Roberts	9	1	35	0
Holding	8.1	2	28	1
Croft	10	0	30	2
Garner	10	2	42	0
Richards	10	0	47	2

Toss won by Australia
Man of the Match: G. S. Chappell
Umpires: C. E. Harvey and R. Harris

BENSON & HEDGES WORLD SERIES CUP
First England v West Indies Match
Sydney, November 28 (England won by 2 runs)
England

D. W. Randall c Parry b Garner	49
*J. M. Brearley c Greenidge b Parry	25
D. I. Gower b Croft	44
G. A. Gooch c & b Parry	2
P. Willey not out	58
I. T. Botham b Garner	11
†D. L. Bairstow c Murray b Garner	0
G. Miller b Roberts	4
G. R. Dilley run out	1
Extras (b4, 1b13)	17
(50 overs) (8 wickets)	211

Did not bat: D. L. Underwood, R. G. D. Willis

Fall of Wickets:
1–79 2–88 3–91 4–160 5–195 6–195 7–210 8–211

Bowling

Roberts	9	0	37	1
Holding	9	0	47	0
Croft	10	0	34	1
Garner	10	0	31	3
Parry	10	0	35	2
Kallicharran	2	0	10	0

West Indies

C. G. Greenidge c Willis b Miller	42
D. L. Haynes b Dilley	4
L. G. Rowe lbw b Willis	60
A. I. Kallicharran run out	44
*C. H. Lloyd c Brearley b Willis	4
†D. L. Murray c Gower b Underwood	3
D. R. Parry b Underwood	4
A. M. E. Roberts c Randall b Underwood	16
J. Garner not out	8
M. A. Holding c Gower b Underwood	0
C. E. H. Croft b Botham	3
Extras (b1, 1b7)	8
(47 overs)	196

Fall of Wickets:
1–19 2–68 3–132 4–143 5–144 6–155 7–177 8–185 9–186

Bowling

Dilley	6	2	21	1
Botham	7	1	26	1
Underwood	10	0	44	4
Miller	10	0	33	1
Willey	8	0	29	0
Willis	6	0	35	2

Umpires: A. Watson and C. E. Harvey
Toss won by West Indies
Man of the Match: P. Willey

BENSON & HEDGES WORLD SERIES CUP
First Australia v England Match
Melbourne, December 8 (England won by 3 wickets)
Australia

J. M. Wiener b Botham	7
B. M. Laird lbw b Dilley	7
A. R. Border c Willey b Dilley	29
*G. S. Chappell c Gooch b Willey	92
K. J. Hughes st Bairstow b Gooch	23
K. D. Walters c Randall b Gooch	12
†R. W. Marsh c Bairstow b Willey	14
R. J. Bright c Gooch b Willey	1
D. K. Lillee not out	13
R. M. Hogg c Brearley b Underwood	1
Extras (b1, lb5, nb2)	8
(50 overs) (9 wickets)	207

Did not bat: J. R. Thomson

Fall of Wickets:
1–15 2–15 3–73 4–114 5–145 6–184 7–193 8–193 9–207

Bowling

Dilley	10	1	30	2
Botham	9	2	27	1
Willis	7	0	28	0
Gooch	6	0	32	2
Underwood	10	0	49	1
Willey	8	0	33	3

England

D. W. Randall lbw b Bright	28
G. Boycott c Lillee b Hogg	68
P. Willey c Marsh b Hogg	37
D. I. Gower c Marsh b Lillee	17
G. A. Gooch run out	1
I. T. Botham c Walters b Hogg	10
*J. M. Brearley c Marsh b Lillee	27
†D. L. Bairstow not out	15
G. R. Dilley not out	0
Extras (lb3, nb3)	6
(49 overs) (7 wickets)	209

Did not bat: D. L. Underwood, R. G. D. Willis

Fall of Wickets:
1–71 2–134 3–137 4–138 5–148 6–183 7–205

Bowling

Lillee	10	1	36	2
Hogg	10	2	26	3
Thomson	10	1	49	0
Chappell	8	0	40	0
Bright	9	1	40	1
Walters	2	0	12	0

Toss won by England
Man of the Match: G. S. Chappell
Umpires: R. A. French and W. J. Copeland

BENSON & HEDGES WORLD SERIES CUP
Second Australia v West Indies Match
Melbourne, December 9 (West Indies won by 80 runs)
West Indies

C. G. Greenidge c Marsh b Lillee	11
D. L. Haynes c Marsh b Thomson	80
I. V. A. Richards not out	153
A. I. Kallicharran not out	16
Extras (b1, 1b10)	11
(48 overs) (2 wickets)	271

Did not bat: L. G. Rowe, C. L. King, *†D. L. Murray, D. R. Parry, A. M. E. Roberts, J. Garner, M. A. Holding

Fall of Wickets:
1–28 2–233

Bowling

Lillee	10	1	48	1
Hogg	10	1	50	0
Chappell	4	0	24	0
Thomson	8	0	43	1
Bright	6	0	29	0
Hookes	1	0	10	0
Border	7	0	40	0
Wiener	2	0	16	0

Australia

B. M. Laird b Holding	7
J. M. Wiener c & b Parry	27
A. R. Border run out	44
*G. S. Chappell c Richards b King	31
K. J. Hughes b Holding	12
D. W. Hookes c Murray b Roberts	9
†R. W. Marsh c Rowe b Roberts	13
R. J. Bright not out	19
D. K. Lillee b King	19
R. M. Hogg not out	3
Extras (1b6, b1)	7
(48 overs) (8 wickets)	191

Did not bat: J. R. Thomson

Fall of Wickets:
1–16 2–54 3–102 4–119 5–128 6–147 7–151 8–185

Bowling

Roberts	8	1	33	2
Holding	10	2	29	2
Garner	10	1	26	0
King	10	0	40	2
Parry	10	0	56	1

Toss won by Australia
Man of the Match: I. V. A. Richards
Umpires: K. J. Carmody and R. V. Whitehead

BENSON & HEDGES WORLD SERIES CUP
Second Australia v England Match
Sydney, December 11 (England won by 72 runs)
England

D. W. Randall run out	42
G. Boycott b Lillee	105
P. Willey c Walker b Chappell	64
D. I. Gower c Wiener b Lillee	7
G. A. Gooch b Thomson	11
I. T. Botham c Walters b Lillee	5
†D. L. Bairstow c sub (Hookes) b Lillee	18
*J. M. Brearley not out	2
Extras (lb6, nb3, w1)	10
(49 overs) (7 wickets)	264

Did not bat: D. L. Underwood, G. R. Dilley, R. G. D. Willis

Fall of Wickets:
1–78 2–196 3–220 4–236 5–242 6–245 7–264

Bowling

Lillee	10	0	56	4
Thomson	9	0	53	1
Walker	10	1	30	0
Laughlin	8	0	39	0
Border	4	0	24	0
Chappell	5	0	28	1
Walters	3	0	24	0

Australia

J. M. Wiener st Bairstow b Willey	14
W. M. Darling c Randall b Willis	20
A. R. Border b Willey	1
*G. S. Chappell run out	0
K. J. Hughes c Bairstow b Willis	1
K. D. Walters c Bairstow b Botham	34
†R. W. Marsh b Dilley	12
T. J. Laughlin c Gooch b Randall	74
D. K. Lillee b Botham	14
J. R. Thomson run out	0
M. H. N. Walker not out	9
Extras (lb10, w2, nb1)	13
(47.2 overs)	192

Fall of Wickets:
1–33 2–36 3–37 4–38 5–39 6–63 7–115 8–146 9–147

Bowling

Dilley	9	0	29	1
Botham	10	1	36	2
Willis	10	1	32	2
Willey	5	0	18	2
Underwood	6	1	29	0
Gooch	7	0	33	0
Randall	0.2	0	2	1

Toss won by England
Man of the Match: G. Boycott
Umpires: J. Collins and J. Stevens

160

BENSON & HEDGES WORLD SERIES CUP
Third Australia v West Indies Match
Sydney, December 21 (Australia won by 7 runs)
Australia

J. M. Wiener c Lloyd b Holding	7
B. M. Laird c Rowe b Roberts	1
A. R. Border c Murray b Garner	17
*G. S. Chappell c Lloyd b Richards	24
K. J. Hughes c Roberts b King	13
I. M. Chappell not out	63
†R. W. Marsh run out	33
G. R. Lillee not out	12
Extras (lb4, nb2)	6
(50 overs) (6 wickets)	176

Did not bat: G. Dymock, L. S. Pascoe, R. M. Hogg

Fall of Wickets:
1–1 2–11 3–28 4–44 5–94 6–160

Bowling

Roberts	10	1	28	1
Holding	10	1	33	1
King	10	0	38	1
Garner	10	2	34	1
Richards	8	0	35	1
Lloyd	2	0	2	0

West Indies

C. G. Greenidge c Marsh b Lillee	33
D. L. Haynes c I. Chappell b Lillee	0
I. V. A. Richards c Hogg b Dymock	62
A. I. Kallicharran b Pascoe	19
L. G. Rowe c Border b G. Chappell	5
*C. H. Lloyd c Wiener b Dymock	0
C. L. King c Marsh b G. Chappell	9
†D. L. Murray not out	17
A. M. E. Roberts lbw b Pascoe	8
J. Garner c G. Chappell b Lillee	2
M. A. Holding b Lillee	0
Extras (lb8, nb6)	14
(42.5 overs)	169

.*Fall of Wickets:*
1–7 2–74 3–112 4–124 5–139 6–144 7–158 8–169

Bowling

Lillee	8.5	0	28	4
Pascoe	10	1	38	2
Hogg	10	3	47	0
Dymock	10	1	28	2
G.S. Chappell	4	0	14	2

Toss won by West Indies
Man of the Match: I. M. Chappell
Umpires: M. W. Johnson and C. E. Harvey

BENSON & HEDGES WORLD SERIES CUP
Second England v West Indies Match

Brisbane, December 23 (West Indies won by 9 wickets)
England

D. W. Randall c Lloyd b Roberts	0
G. Boycott c sub (Marshall) b Holding	68
P. Willey run out	34
D. I. Gower c Holding b Roberts	59
G. A. Gooch b Garner	17
I. T. Botham lbw b Holding	4
†D. L. Bairstow c Lloyd b Roberts	12
*J. M. Brearley not out	9
G. R. Dilley b Garner	0
Extras (lb8, w5, nb1)	14
(50 overs) (8 wickets)	217

Did not bat: D. L. Underwood, R. G. D. Willis

Fall of Wickets:
1–0 2–70 3–167 4–174 5–191 6–205 7–209 8–217

Bowling				
Roberts	10	3	26	3
Holding	10	1	44	2
Garner	10	0	37	2
Richards	10	0	44	0
King	10	0	52	0

West Indies

C. G. Greenidge not out	85
D. L. Haynes c Underwood b Gooch	41
I. V. A. Richards not out	85
Extras (lb4, nb3)	7
(46.5 overs) (1 wicket)	218

Did not bat: A. I. Kallicharran, L. G. Rowe, *C. H. Lloyd, C. L. King, †D. L. Murray, A. M. E. Roberts, J. Garner, M. A. Holding

Fall of Wickets:
1–109

Bowling				
Botham	10	1	39	0
Dilley	8	1	25	0
Willis	10	2	27	0
Underwood	9	0	43	0
Willey	6	0	39	0
Gooch	3.5	0	38	1

Toss won by West Indies
Man of the Match: C. G. Greenidge
Umpires: C. E. Harvey and M. W. Johnson

BENSON & HEDGES WORLD SERIES CUP
Third Australia v England Match

Sydney. December 26. (England won by 4 wickets)

Australia

B. M. Laird b Botham	6
J. M. Wiener c Bairstow b Botham	2
A. R. Border c Gower b Gocch	22
*G. S. Chappell run out	52
K. J. Hughes b Willis	23
I. M. Chappell not out	60
†R. W. Marsh c Bairstow b Dilley	10
D. K. Lillee not out	2
Extras (b3, lb10, nb4)	17
(47 overs) (6 wickets)	194

Did not bat: R. M. Hogg, G. Dymock, L. S. Pascoe

Fall of wickets:
1–5 2–21 3–50 4–109 5–135 6–179

Bowling

Dilley	10	1	32	1
Botham	9	1	33	2
Willis	10	1	38	1
Underwood	10	2	36	0
Gooch	8	0	38	1

England

G. A. Gooch lbw b Hogg	29
G. Boycott not out	86
P. Willey b Pascoe	51
D. I. Gower c Marsh b Hogg	2
D. W. Randall c G. Chappell b Pascoe	1
I. T. Botham lbw b Hogg	6
*J. M. Brearley c Marsh b Hogg	0
†D. L. Bairstow not out	7
Extras (lb1, w1, nb11)	13
(45.1 overs) (6 wickets)	195

Did not bat: G. R. Dilley, R. G. D. Willis, D. L. Underwood

Fall of wickets:
1–41 2–152 3–157 4–170 5–179 6–179

Bowling

Lillee	10	0	47	0
Pascoe	10	2	28	2
Hogg	10	0	46	4
Dymock	10	1	38	0
G. Chappell	5.1	0	23	0

Toss won by Australia
Man of the Match: G. Boycott
Umpires: P. M. Cronin and R. Isherwood

BENSON & HEDGES WORLD SERIES CUP
Third England v West Indies Match

Melbourne. January 12. (Abandoned without a ball bowled—one point each)

BENSON & HEDGES WORLD SERIES CUP
Fourth Australia v England Match

Sydney. January 14. (England won by 2 wickets)

Australia

J. M. Wiener st Bairstow b Emburey	33
R. B. McCosker c Brearley b Willey	41
I. M. Chappell c Randall b Emburey	8
*G. S. Chappell c Randall b Stevenson	34
K. J. Hughes c Larkins b Lever	34
A. R. Border c Bairstow b Lever	0
†R. W. Marsh c Bairstow b Stevenson	0
D. K. Lillee lbw b Stevenson	0
G. Dymock run out	0
J. R. Thomson not out	3
L. S. Pascoe b Stevenson	5
Extras (lb1, w3, nb1)	5
(48.4 overs)	163

Fall of wickets:
1–74 2–82 3–89 4–148 5–149 6–150 7–150 8–152 9–155

Bowling

Lever	9	1	11	2
Botham	7	0	33	0
Gooch	3	0	13	0
Stevenson	9.4	0	33	4
Emburey	10	1	33	2
Willey	10	0	35	1

England

G. A. Gooch c McCosker b Pascoe	69
W. Larkins c Thomson b Lillee	5
P. Willey lbw b Lillee	0
D. I. Gower c Marsh b Lillee	3
*J. M. Brearley b G. Chappell	5
D. W. Randall c Pascoe b G. Chappell	0
I. T. Botham b Lillee	0
D. L. Bairstow not out	21
J. E. Emburey c G. Chappell b Dymock	18
G. B. Stevenson not out	28
Extras (nb9, w1, lb5)	15
(48.5 overs) (8 wickets)	164

Did not bat: J. K. Lever

Fall of wickets:
1–31 2–31 3–40 4–51 5–56 6–61 7–105 8–129

Bowling

Thomson	9.5	0	46	0
Dymock	9	1	30	1
Lillee	10	6	12	4
Pascoe	10	0	38	1
G. Chappell	10	3	23	2

Toss won by England
Man of the Match: D. K. Lillee
Umpires: R. Isherwood & R. Whitehead

BENSON & HEDGES WORLD SERIES CUP
Fourth England v West Indies Match
Adelaide, January 16. (West Indies won by 107 runs)
West Indies

C. G. Greenidge c Emburey b Willey	50
D. L. Haynes c Gooch b Stevenson	26
I. V. A. Richards b Botham	88
A. I. Kallicharran c & b Botham	57
C. L. King run out	12
J. Garner not out	7
A. M. E. Roberts not out	0
Extras (b1, lb4, nb1)	6
(50 overs) (5 wickets)	246

Did not bat: *C. H. Lloyd, L. G. Rowe, †D. L. Murray, M. A. Holding

Fall of Wickets:
1–58 2–115 3–224 4–227 5–245

Bowling

Lever	10	1	54	0
Botham	10	0	35	2
Gooch	2	0	22	0
Stevenson	8	1	53	1
Emburey	10	0	39	0
Willey	10	1	37	1

England

G. A. Gooch b King	20
*J. M. Brearley c Murray b Roberts	0
P. Willey c Lloyd b King	5
W. Larkins c Lloyd b King	24
D. I. Gower c sub (Parry) b King	12
D. W. Randall b Roberts	16
I. T. Botham c Haynes b Roberts	22
†D. L. Bairstow not out	23
G. B. Stevenson b Roberts	1
J. E. Emburey c Murray b Roberts	1
J. K. Lever b Garner	11
Extras (lb2, nb1, w1)	4
(42.5 overs)	139

Fall of Wickets:
1–5 2–24 3–31 4–52 5–68 6–98 7–100 8–105 9–109

Bowling

Roberts	10	5	22	5
Holding	7	0	16	0
King	9	3	23	4
Garner	7.5	3	9	1
Richards	7	0	46	0
Kallicharran	2	0	19	0

Toss won by England
Man of the Match: A. M. E. Roberts
Umpires: G. Duperouzal and P. M. Cronin

BENSON & HEDGES WORLD SERIES CUP
Fourth Australia v West Indies Match
Sydney, January 18. (Australia won by 9 runs)
Australia

R. B. McCosker c Lloyd b Holding	95
J. M. Wiener c Gomes b Parry	50
K. J. Hughes b Parry	4
*G. S. Chappell c & b Parry	2
G. N. Yallop b Roberts	11
D. F. Whatmore c Murray b Holding	2
†R. W. Marsh c Lloyd b Roberts	5
D. K. Lillee c Murray b Holding	0
M. H. N. Walker run out	5
G. Dymock not out	4
L. S. Pascoe b Holding	0
Extras (b1, 1b10, w1)	12
(48.3 overs)	190

Fall of Wickets:
1–103 2–124 3–134 4–161 5–166 6–177 7–177 8–177 9–190

Bowling

Holding	9.3	2	17	4
Croft	10	0	22	0
King	9	0	40	0
Roberts	10	0	38	2
Parry	10	0	61	3

West Indies

L. G. Rowe lbw b Dymock	3
D. L. Haynes c Marsh b Lillee	1
†D. A. Murray c Chappell b Pascoe	35
A. I. Kallicharran lbw b Chappell	66
*C. H. Lloyd not out	34
C. L. King lbw b Walker	0
H. A. Gomes lbw b Lillee	4
D. R. Parry b Pascoe	9
A. M. E. Roberts c Marsh b Lillee	2
M. A. Holding c & b Pascoe	8
C. E. H. Croft c Lillee b Chappell	8
Extras (nb8, 1b3)	11
(49.1 overs)	181

Fall of Wickets:
1–4 2–8 3–91 4–134 5–134 6–140 7–152 8–157 9–166

Bowling

Lillee	10	3	17	3
Dymock	10	2	18	1
Walker	10	2	46	1
Pascoe	10	0	34	3
Chappell	7.1	0	37	2
Wiener	2	0	18	0

Toss won by Australia
Man of the Match: R. B. McCosker
Umpires: K. Carmody and A. Watson

BENSON & HEDGES WORLD SERIES CUP
FIRST FINAL England v West Indies
Melbourne. January 20. (West Indies won by 2 runs)
West Indies

C. G. Greenidge c Larkins b Botham	80
D. L. Haynes c Bairstow b Willis	9
I. V. A. Richards c Bairstow b Dilley	23
A. I. Kallicharran b Botham	42
*C. H. Lloyd b Botham	4
C. L. King not out	31
†D. L. Murray c Bairstow b Dilley	4
A. M. E. Roberts run out	1
J. Garner run out	3
M. A. Holding not out	5
Extras (lb11, w1, nb1)	13
(50 overs) (8 wickets)	215

Did not bat: C. E. H. Croft

Fall of wickets:
1–17 2–66 3–161 4–168 5–168 6–181 7–183 8–197

Bowling				
Willis	10	1	51	1
Botham	10	2	33	3
Emburey	10	0	31	0
Dilley	10	0	39	2
Willey	10	0	48	0

England

G. A. Gooch c King b Holding	9
G. Boycott c Haynes b Roberts	35
P. Willey run out	51
D. I. Gower c Holding b Roberts	10
W. Larkins run out	34
I. T. Botham c Lloyd b Roberts	19
*J. M. Brearley not out	25
†D. L. Bairstow run out	4
Extras (b12, lb12, w1, nb1)	26
(50 overs) (7 wickets)	213

Did not bat: J. E. Emburey, G. R. Dilley, R. G. D. Willis

Fall of wickets:
1–13 2–74 3–96 4–152 5–164 6–190 7–213

Bowling				
Roberts	10	1	30	3
Holding	10	1	43	1
Garner	10	1	27	0
Croft	10	1	23	0
King	4	0	30	0
Richards	6	1	34	0

Toss won by England
Umpires: R. C. Bailhache and C. E. Harvey
Attendance: 30,196

BENSON & HEDGES WORLD SERIES CUP
SECOND FINAL England v West Indies

Sydney, January 22. (West Indies won by 8 wickets)

England

G. A. Gooch lbw b Garner	23
G. Boycott c Greenidge b Roberts	63
P. Willey b Garner	3
D. I. Gower c Murray b Holding	27
W. Larkins b Croft	14
I. T. Botham c King b Roberts	37
†D. L. Bairstow not out	18
*J. M. Brearley run out	4
J. E. Emburey run out	6
Extras (b1, lb11, nb1)	13
(50 overs) (8 wickets)	208

Did not bat: G. R. Dilley, R. G. D. Willis

Fall of wickets:
1–40 2–54 3–118 4–126 5–155 6–188 7–194 8–208

Bowling

Roberts	10	3	31	2
Holding	10	1	34	1
Croft	10	3	29	1
Garner	10	0	44	2
Richards	3	0	19	0
King	7	1	38	0

West Indies

C. G. Greenidge not out	98
D. L. Haynes lbw b Botham	17
I. V. A. Richards c Botham b Willey	65
A. I. Kallicharran not out	8
Extras (b5, lb10, w5, nb1)	21
(47.3 overs) (2 wickets)	209

Did not bat: *C. H. Lloyd, C. L. King, †D. L. Murray, A. M. E. Roberts, J. Garner, M. A. Holding, C. E. H. Croft

Fall of wickets:
1–61 2–180

Bowling

Willis	10	0	35	0
Dilley	7	0	37	0
Botham	10	1	28	0
Emburey	9.3	0	48	0
Willey	10	2	35	1
Gooch	1	0	5	0

Toss won by England
Umpires: A. F. Crafter and M. G. O'Connell
Player of the Finals: C. G. Greenidge
Player of the Series: I. V. A. Richards
Attendance: 20,840
Prize-money: West Indies $32,000, England $16,000

(4) THE AVERAGES

AUSTRALIA
TEST MATCH AVERAGES v ENGLAND

(Batting)

	M	Inns	NO	Runs	HS	Av
G. S. Chappell	3	6	2	317	114	79.25
I. M. Chappell	2	4	1	152	75	50.66
A. R. Border	3	5	1	199	115	49.75
K. J. Hughes	3	5	0	183	99	36.60
B. M. Laird	2	4	0	132	74	33.00
J. M. Wiener	2	4	0	104	58	26.00
R. B. McCosker	2	4	0	77	41	19.25
R. W. Marsh	3	4	0	70	42	17.50
G. Dymock	3	4	1	48	20*	16.00
R. J. Bright	1	2	0	29	17	14.50
D. K. Lillee	3	4	0	50	19	12.50
P. M. Toohey	1	2	0	22	19	11.00
J. R. Thomson	1	2	1	9	8	9.00
L. S. Pascoe	2	2	2	11	10*	—

Also batted: A. A. Mallett, 25; J. D. Higgs, 2

(Bowling)

	O	M	R	W	Av
G. Dymock	130.3	40	260	17	15.29
G. S. Chappell	42	21	66	4	16.50
D. K. Lillee	165.1	41	388	23	16.87
L. S. Pascoe	93.5	17	241	10	24.10
Also bowled					
J. R. Thomson	32	6	100	3	
R. J. Bright	25	11	36	1	
A. A. Mallett	49	10	149	1	
A. R. Border	6	0	23	0	
J. M. Wiener	8	3	22	0	
J. D. Higgs	1	0	3	0	

AUSTRALIA
TEST MATCH AVERAGES v WEST INDIES

(Batting)

	M	Inns	NO	Runs	HS	Av
B. M. Laird	3	6	0	340	92	56.66
K. J. Hughes	3	6	1	252	130*	50.40
G. S. Chappell	3	6	0	270	124	45.00
D. W. Hookes	1	2	0	80	43	40.00
R. B. McCosker	1	2	0	47	33	23.50
A. R. Border	3	6	0	118	54	19.66
J. M. Wiener	2	4	0	75	40	18.75
R. J. Bright	1	2	1	15	13	15.00
R. W. Marsh	3	6	1	57	23*	11.40
R. M. Hogg	2	3	0	33	14	11.00
L. S. Pascoe	1	2	1	10	5*	10.00
G. Dymock	2	4	0	36	17	9.00
P. M. Toohey	1	2	0	17	10	8.50
A. A. Mallett	1	2	0	12	12	6.00
D. K. Lillee	3	5	0	28	16	5.60
I. M. Chappell	1	2	0	6	4	3.00

Also batted: J. D. Higgs, 0* and 0*; J. R. Thomson, 0*.

(Bowling)

	O	M	R	W	Av
J. R. Thomson	27	6	93	4	23.25
G. Dymock	92.5	16	289	11	26.27
G. S. Chappell	17	4	28	1	28.00
D. K. Lillee	120.1	24	365	12	30.41
J. D. Higgs	34.4	4	122	3	40.66
A. A. Mallett	65	12	211	4	52.75
L. R. Pascoe	40.3	4	183	3	61.00
R. M. Hogg	36	8	125	2	62.50
R. J. Bright	36	12	105	1	105.00
Also bowled:					
A. R. Border	9	3	29	1	
D. W. Hookes	5	2	15	0	
K. J. Hughes	1	1	0	0	
P. M. Toohey	0.2	0	4	0	

ENGLAND
TEST MATCH AVERAGES V AUSTRALIA

(Batting)

	M	Inns	NO	Runs	HS	Av
G. A. Gooch	2	4	0	172	99	43.00
G. R. Dilley	2	4	2	80	38*	40.00
I. T. Botham	3	6	1	187	119*	37.40
G. Boycott	3	6	1	176	99*	35.20
J. M. Brearley	3	6	1	171	64	34.20
D. I. Gower	3	6	1	152	98*	30.40
R. W. Taylor	3	6	0	102	32	17.00
J. K. Lever	1	2	0	34	22	17.00
G. Miller	1	2	0	33	25	16.50
W. Larkins	1	2	0	28	25	14.00
D. L. Underwood	3	6	0	71	43	11.83
D. W. Randall	2	4	0	26	25	6.50
P. Willey	3	6	0	35	12	5.83
R. G. D. Willis	3	6	0	21	11	3.50

(Bowling)

	O	M	R	W	Av
G. A. Gooch	19	6	36	2	18.00
I. T. Botham	173.1	62	371	19	19.53
D. L. Underwood	160.2	48	405	13	31.15
J. K. Lever	60.4	18	129	4	32.25
G. R. Dilley	53	5	143	3	47.66
R. G. D. Willis	114	26	224	3	74.66
G. Miller	21	2	66	0	—
P. Willey	19	2	56	0	—

WEST INDIES
TEST MATCH AVERAGES v. AUSTRALIA

(Batting)

	M	I	NO	Runs	HS	Av.
I. V. A. Richards	3	4	0	386	140	96.50
C. H. Lloyd	2	3	0	201	121	67.00
A. I. Kallicharran	3	5	1	202	106	50.50
J. Garner	3	4	1	106	60	35.33
C. G. Greenidge	3	6	1	173	76	34.60
L. G. Rowe	3	5	0	162	50	32.40
D. L. Haynes	3	6	1	139	42	27.80
A. M. E. Roberts	3	4	0	78	54	19.50
D. L. Murray	3	4	0	77	28	19.25
C. L. King	1	2	1	8	8*	8.00
C. E. H. Croft	3	4	2	15	12	7.50
M. A. Holding	3	4	1	22	11	7.33

(Bowling)

	O	M	R	W	Av.
J. Garner	127.4	34	301	14	21.50
M. A. Holding	111	24	319	14	22.78
C. E. H. Croft	121.3	20	378	16	23.62
A. M. E. Roberts	112	20	296	11	26.90
C. L. King	27	7	63	1	63.00
Also bowled:					
A. I. Kallicharran	18	2	32	0	
I. V. A. Richards	2	0	7	0	

ONE-DAY INTERNATIONALS

ENGLAND

(Batting)

	M	Inns	NO	Runs	HS	Av.
G. Boycott	6	6	1	425	105	85.00
P. Willey	9	9	1	303	64	37.87
D. L. Bairstow	9	9	5	118	23*	29.50
G. B. Stevenson	2	2	1	29	28*	29.00
G. A. Gooch	9	9	0	181	69	20.11
D. I. Gower	9	9	0	181	59	20.11
D. W. Randall	7	7	0	136	49	19.42
W. Larkins	4	4	0	77	34	19.25
J. M. Brearley	9	9	3	97	27	16.16
I. T. Botham	9	9	0	114	37	12.66
J. K. Lever	2	1	0	11	11	11.00
J. E. Emburey	4	3	0	25	18	8.33
G. R. Dilley	7	3	1	1	1	0.50

Played in one match: G. Miller 4
R. G. D. Willis played in 7 matches but did not bat.
D. L. Underwood played in 5 matches but did not bat.

(Bowling)

	O	M	R	W	Av.
G. B. Stevenson	17.4	1	86	5	17.20
I. T. Botham	73	8	257	10	25.70
G. R. Dilley	50	4	181	6	30.16
J. K. Lever	19	2	65	2	32.50
D. L. Underwood	35	1	165	5	33.00
P. Willey	67	3	274	8	34.25
J. E. Emburey	39.3	1	159	4	39.75
R. G. D. Willis	53	4	208	5	41.60
G. A. Gooch	22.5	0	133	3	44.33
Also bowled:					
G. Miller	10	0	33	1	
D. W. Randall	0.2	0	2	1	

AUSTRALIA

(Batting)

	M	Inns	NO	Runs	HS	Av
I. M. Chappell	3	3	2	131	63*	131.00
R. B. McCosker	3	3	0	137	95	45.66
G. S. Chappell	8	8	1	309	74*	44.14
K. D. Walters	2	2	0	46	34	23.00
K. J. Hughes	8	8	0	162	52	20.25
R. J. Bright	2	2	1	20	19*	20.00
J. M. Wiener	7	7	0	140	50	20.00
A. R. Border	7	7	0	130	44	18.57
D. K. Lillee	8	7	3	60	19	15.00
R. W. Marsh	8	8	1	105	33	15.00
B. M. Laird	5	5	0	41	20	8.20
M. H. N. Walker	2	2	0	14	9	7.00
G. Dymock	4	2	1	4	4*	4.00
R. M. Hogg	5	2	1	4	3*	4.00
J. R. Thomson	4	2	1	3	3*	3.00
L. R. Pascoe	5	2	0	5	5	2.50

Played in one match: W. M. Darling, 20; T. J. Laughlin, 74; G. N. Yallop, 11; D. F. Whatmore, 2.

(Bowling)

	O	M	R	W	Av
D. K. Lillee	74.5	13	254	20	12.70
L. S. Pascoe	49.3	4	167	12	13.91
G. Dymock	39	5	114	4	28.50
R. M. Hogg	50	6	218	7	31.14
G. S. Chappell	52.2	3	226	7	32.28
A. R. Border	21	0	100	3	33.33
M. H. N. Walker	20	3	76	1	76.00
R. J. Bright	20	1	95	1	95.00
J. R. Thomson	36.5	1	191	2	95.50
K. D. Walters	5	0	36	0	—
J. M. Wiener	4	0	34	0	—
Also bowled:					
T. J. Laughlin	8	0	39	0	
D. W. Hookes	1	0	10	0	

WEST INDIES

(Batting)

	M	Inns	NO	Runs	HS	Av
I. V. A. Richards	8	8	3	545	153*	109.00
C. G. Greenidge	8	8	2	404	98*	67.33
A. I. Kallicharran	9	8	2	301	66	50.16
D. L. Haynes	9	9	0	207	80	23.00
C. L. King	8	5	1	81	31*	20.25
D. L. Murray	8	4	1	51	27	17.00
C. H. Lloyd	8	5	1	58	34*	14.50
A. M. E. Roberts	9	6	1	43	16	8.60
J. Garner	8	5	2	25	8*	8.33
D. R. Parry	3	2	0	13	9	6.50
C. E. H. Croft	5	3	1	11	8	5.50
L. G. Rowe	5	2	0	8	5	4.00
M. A. Holding	9	5	1	15	8	3.75

Played in one match: H. A. Gomes, 4; D. A. Murray, 35.

(Bowling)

	O	M	R	W	Av
A. M. E. Roberts	86	15	280	19	14.73
M. A. Holding	83.4	10	291	12	24.25
D. R. Parry	30	0	152	6	25.33
J. Garner	77.5	9	250	9	27.77
C. E. H. Croft	50	4	138	4	34.50
C. L. King	59	4	261	7	37.28
I. V. A. Richards	44	1	225	3	75.00
A. I. Kallicharran	4	0	29	0	–
Also bowled:					
C. H. Lloyd	2	0	2	0	

ENGLAND TOUR

CENTURIES FOR:

G. Boycott	(3)	110	v	South Australia	Adelaide
		105	v	AUSTRALIA (Second B & H World Series Cup)	Sydney (not first-class)
		101*	v	Tasmania	Hobart
I. T. Botham	(2)	119*	v	AUSTRALIA (Third Test)	Melbourne
		114	v	INDIA (Jubilee Test)	Bombay
G. A. Gooch	(2)	124	v	Combined Universities	Adelaide (not first-class)
		115	v	Queensland	Brisbane
P. Willey	(1)	101*	v	Queensland	Brisbane

CENTURIES AGAINST:

A. R. Border	115	v	ENGLAND (First Test)	Perth
G. S. Chappell	114	v	ENGLAND (Third Test)	Melbourne

5 WICKETS IN AN INNINGS FOR:

I. T. Botham	(4)	6–78 5–98	v	AUSTRALIA (First Test)	Perth
		6–58 7–48	v	INDIA (Jubilee Test)	Bombay
D. L. Underwood	(2)	8–41	v	Combined Universities	Adelaide (not first-class)
		7–66	v	Tasmania	Hobart

5 WICKETS IN AN INNINGS AGAINST:

D. K. Lillee	(2)	6–60 5–78	for AUSTRALIA (Third Test)	Melbourne
G. Dymock	(1)	6–34	for AUSTRALIA (First Test)	Perth
K. D. Ghavri	(1)	5–52	for INDIA (Jubilee Test)	Bombay
G. Kirkwood	(1)	5–52	for Combined Universities	Adelaide (not first-class)
C. G. Rackemann	(1)	5–25	for Queensland	Brisbane

WEST INDIES TOUR

CENTURIES FOR:

A. I. Kallicharran	(3)	138	v	Tasmania	Launceston
		123	v	Invitation XI	Devonport
		106	v	AUSTRALIA (Third Test)	Adelaide
I. V. A. Richards	(3)	153*	v	AUSTRALIA (Second B & H World Series Cup)	Melbourne (not first-class)
		140	v	AUSTRALIA (First Test)	Brisbane
		127	v	Invitation XI	Devonport
H. A. Gomes	(1)	137*	v	Tasmania	Launceston
C. H. Lloyd	(1)	121	v	AUSTRALIA (Third Test)	Adelaide
D. L. Murray	(1)	103	v	South Australia	Adelaide

CENTURIES AGAINST:

G. S. Chappell	124	for AUSTRALIA (First Test)	Brisbane
K. J. Hughes	130*	for AUSTRALIA (First Test)	Brisbane
R. S. Langer	137	for Western Australia	Perth
K. S. McEwan	112	for Western Australia	Perth

5 WICKETS IN AN INNINGS FOR:

C. E. H. Croft	(2)	5–49	v	Invitation XI	Devonport
		5–65	v	Tasmania	Launceston
J. Garner	(1)	5–43	v	Tasmania	Launceston
M. D. Marshall	(1)	5–62	v	Geelong & Districts	Geelong (not first-class)
A. M. E. Roberts	(1)	5–22	v	ENGLAND (Fourth B & H World Series Cup)	Adelaide (not first-class)

5 WICKETS IN AN INNINGS AGAINST:

T. M. Alderman	5–47	for Western Australia	Perth
G. Dymock	5–104	for AUSTRALIA (Third Test)	Adelaide
R. M. Hogg	6–95	for South Australia	Adelaide
D. K. Lillee	5–78	for AUSTRALIA (Third Test)	Adelaide

(5) TOUR NOTES

ENGLAND

ENGLAND XI v TASMANIA at Hobart
G. Boycott's 101* on November 30th was his 116th first-class century. Play was abandoned at lunch on the second day due to strong winds.

ENGLAND XI v SOUTH AUSTRALIA at Adelaide
G. Boycott's 110 on December 4th was his 117th first-class century, equalling the number of centuries scored by D. G. Bradman.

FIRST TEST MATCH AUSTRALIA v ENGLAND at Perth
G. R. Dilley, aged 20 years 210 days, became the youngest England Test player since D. B. Close (18 years 149 days) v New Zealand in 1949. M. W. Gatting was 20 years 226 days when he made his début v Pakistan at Karachi in 1977-78.

D. K. Lillee in his 19th Test became the eighth Australian bowler to take 100 wickets against England when he dismissed J. M. Brearley in the first innings. The other bowlers to have achieved this feat are: H. Trumble 141, M. A. Noble 115, R. R. Lindwall 114, C. V. Grimmett 106, G. Giffen 103, W. J. O'Reilly 102 and C. T. B. Turner 101.

J. R. Thomson in his 34th Test took his 150th Test wicket when he dismissed G. Miller in the first innings.

A. R. Border broke the world Test record for the most Test match runs in the year following his Test début by aggregating 1070 runs in 13 Tests (26 innings). The previous Australian record was held by H. R. Collins with 968 runs in 11 Tests (17 innings) from December 1920. The previous world record was held by H. Sutcliffe (1037 runs in 10 Tests, 14 innings) from June 1924. Border's innings of 115 was his third Test century.

I. T. Botham had match figures of 11-176, the best match figures recorded in a Perth Test match. The only other bowlers to take 10 wickets in a Test Match at Perth are B. S. Bedi and R. M. Hogg.

G. Boycott became the first batsman ever to score 99 not out in Test cricket and in so doing is only the second batsman to score 99 twice in Tests, the other being M. J. K. Smith.

G. Boycott became the third England batsman to carry his bat through an innings against Australia. The others were:
R. Abel 132* out of 307 at Sydney 1891-92
L. Hutton 156* out of 272 at Adelaide 1950-51

ENGLAND XI v QUEENSLAND at Brisbane
I. T. Botham captained England for the first time.
J. E. Emburey scored his maiden half-century in first-class cricket.

SECOND TEST MATCH AUSTRALIA v ENGLAND at Sydney

I. M. Chappell became the 9th Australian to score 2,000 runs in Test matches v England when he reached 14 in his first-innings score of 42. The others to achieve this feat are:

D. G. Bradman	5028
C. Hill	2660
R. N. Harvey	2416
V. T. Trumper	2263
W. M. Lawry	2233
S. E. Gregory	2193
W. W. Armstrong	2172
A. R. Morris	2080

G. S. Chappell in the first innings was dismissed for the 13th time in 50 innings by D. L. Underwood.

D. L. Underwood, when he dismissed J. M. Wiener in the second innings, became the fifth English bowler to take 100 wickets v Australia in Test cricket. The others are:

W. Rhodes	109	(Av. 24.00)
S. F. Barnes	106	(Av. 21.58)
A. V. Bedser	104	(Av. 27.49)
R. Peel	102	(Av. 16.81)

THIRD TEST AUSTRALIA v ENGLAND at Melbourne

P. Cronin, one of the umpires, had – previously to this Test match – only stood in four first-class matches spread over three seasons.

G. A. Gooch's 99 was his highest Test score and the 35th case of a batsman scoring 99 in a Test match, the third case in this series. He provided the first instance of a batsman being run out for 99 in England v Australia Test matches; others who have been so dismissed in Test cricket are:

W. A. Brown	Australia v India, Melbourne 1947-48
A. R. Morris	Australia v South Africa, Melbourne 1952-53
J. E. F. Beck	New Zealand v South Africa, Cape Town 1953-54
R. B. Kanhai	West Indies v India, Madras 1958-59
M. L. Jaisimha	India v Pakistan, Kanpur 1960-61
Mushtaq Mohammad	Pakistan v England, Karachi 1972-73.

D. K. Lillee took his 200th wicket in Test cricket when he bowled J. K. Lever in the first innings. This landmark was achieved in his 39th Test.

G. S. Chappell, when he had scored 30 of his first-innings 114, became the tenth Australian to reach 2,000 runs in Test cricket against England. His 114 was his 16th Test century, and seventh v England.

I. T. Botham's 119* was his 5th Test hundred, and first against Australia.

D. K. Lillee took 11–138 (6–60 and 5–78) in the match and was declared man of the series.

INDIA v ENGLAND at Bombay. The Jubilee Test
On February 16th a rest day was declared due to a total solar eclipse that occurred at 3.39pm.

In India's first innings R. W. Taylor equalled Wasim Bari's Test record of 7 catches in an innings with his dismissal of D. R. Doshi. Wasim Bari's record was set for Pakistan v New Zealand at Auckland in 1979.

I. T. Botham's 114 was his sixth Test century and second successive Test century.

I. T. Botham's final match figures of 48.5–14–106–13 have only been bettered in India by: J. M. Patel 14–124 for India v Australia at Kanpur 1959-60. His 6–58 and 7–48 were the 13th and 14th time he has taken 5 wickets in an innings in only his 25th Test match. He became the first Englishman to take 13 or more wickets in a Test match since D. L. Underwood v Pakistan at Lord's in 1974.

R. W. Taylor's 10 catches in the match are a new world Test record, beating G. R. Langley's 8 catches and one stumping for Australia v England at Lord's in 1956.

WEST INDIES

WEST INDIANS v INVITATION XI at Devonport
I. V. A. Richards and A. I. Kallicharran put on 241 for the 3rd wicket—a record for a West Indies side in Australia. The previous record of 190 unbroken v Tasmania at Hobart in 1975-76 was also held by Richards and Kallicharran.

FIRST TEST MATCH. AUSTRALIA v WEST INDIES at Brisbane
D. L. Murray in his 52nd Test match captained West Indies throughout a Test for the first time.

R. W. Marsh in his 53rd Test match became the third wicket-keeper to make 200 dismissals in Test cricket when he caught D. L. Haynes in the first innings. The others are:
A. P. E. Knott 252 victims in 89 Tests
T. G. Evans 219 victims in 91 Tests

I. V. A. Richards' 140 was his 9th Test hundred.

J. Garner's 60 was his maiden half-century in both Test and first-class cricket.

J. Garner (60) and C. E. H. Croft (2*) put on 56 for the 10th wicket—a record for Australia v West Indies Tests.

G. S. Chappell's 124 was his 15th Test hundred and 56th first-class century.

K. J. Hughes's 130* was his 3rd Test century and highest Test score.

WEST INDIANS v TASMANIA at Launceston
The West Indies score of 545 for 5 declared was their highest score ever against an Australian state.

SECOND TEST MATCH. AUSTRALIA v WEST INDIES at Melbourne
A. M. E. Roberts' 54 was his maiden half-century in Test cricket.

West Indies' victory was their first-ever at Melbourne in a Test match.

WEST INDIANS v WESTERN AUSTRALIA at Perth
R. S. Langer (137) and K. S. McEwan (112) put on 207 in 167 minutes for Western Australia's fourth wicket.

THIRD TEST MATCH. AUSTRALIA v WEST INDIES at Adelaide
C. H. Lloyd's 121 was his 12th Test century. Whilst batting he struck a seagull 35 yards from the wicket with a powerful off-drive. The stunned bird was carried off the field by D. K. Lillee, and later recovered.

A. I. Kallicharran, when he had scored 35 in his innings of 106 (his 12th Test century), became the 6th West Indian to score 4,000 runs in Test cricket, the others being: R. B. Kanhai, C. H. Lloyd, R. C. Fredericks, G. S. Sobers and E. D. Weekes.

West Indies won their first series in Australia 2–0 when they beat Australia by 408 runs. This was the 6th biggest margin in terms of runs ever recorded in a Test match. It was also Australia's heaviest defeat since losing by 675 runs to England at Brisbane in 1928-29.

ENGLAND TOUR AVERAGES

Including the Jubilee Test
(Batting)

	M	Inns	NO	Runs	HS	Av
G. A. Gooch	7	14	3	639	115	58.09
G. Boycott	8	15	4	599	110	54.45
G. Miller	4	6	2	203	71	50.75
I. T. Botham	6	9	1	323	119*	40.37
G. R. Dilley	5	6	3	101	38*	33.66
G. B. Stevenson	4	5	2	91	33	30.33
J. M. Brearley	7	11	1	302	81	30.20
P. Willey	6	12	3	269	101*	29.89
D. I. Gower	9	15	2	354	98*	27.23
D. W. Randall	6	10	0	250	97	25.00
R. W. Taylor	8	11	1	227	47*	22.70
W. Larkins	6	10	1	190	90	21.11
J. E. Emburey	3	4	0	71	50	17.75
J. K. Lever	7	7	2	75	22	15.00
D. L. Underwood	6	8	0	88	43	11.00
D. L. Bairstow	2	2	0	13	12	6.50
R. G. D. Willis	4	6	0	21	11	3.50
M. Hendrick	1	1	0	1	1	1.00

(Bowling)

	O	M	R	W	Av.
I. T. Botham	242	81	532	34	15.64
D. L. Underwood	260	81	609	25	24.36
G. B. Stevenson	87	13	307	11	27.97
G. R. Dilley	88.1	11	243	7	34.71
G. A. Gooch	45	13	113	3	37.66
J. K. Lever	235.4	55	622	16	38.87
J. E. Emburey	111.2	25	282	7	40.29
P. Willey	111	17	332	7	47.43
G. Miller	106	20	268	5	53.60
R. G. D. Willis	129	30	252	3	84.00
Also bowled:					
G. Boycott	4	0	19	0	
W. Larkins	6	0	15	0	
M. Hendrick	4	1	14	0	